MW00810742

# What Makes a Social Crisis?

## The Societalization of Social Problems

Jeffrey C. Alexander

polity

Copyright © Jeffrey C. Alexander 2019

The right of Jeffrey C. Alexander to be identified as Author of this Work has been asserted in accordance with the UK Copyright, Designs and Patents Act 1988.

First published in 2019 by Polity Press

Polity Press
65 Bridge Street
Cambridge CB2 1UR, UK

Polity Press
101 Station Landing
Suite 300
Medford, MA 02155, USA

All rights reserved. Except for the quotation of short passages for the purpose of criticism and review, no part of this publication may be reproduced, stored in a retrieval system or transmitted, in any form or by any means, electronic, mechanical, photocopying, recording or otherwise, without the prior permission of the publisher.

ISBN-13: 978-1-5095-3824-9
ISBN-13: 978-1-5095-3825-6 (pb)

A catalogue record for this book is available from the British Library.

Library of Congress Cataloging-in-Publication Data
Names: Alexander, Jeffrey C., 1947- author.
Title: What makes a social crisis? : the societalization of social problems / Jeffrey C. Alexander.
Description: Medford, MA : Polity Press, [2019] | Includes bibliographical references and index.
Identifiers: LCCN 2019004021 (print) | LCCN 2019011468 (ebook) | ISBN 9781509538263 (Epub) | ISBN 9781509538881 (Epdf) | ISBN 9781509538249 (hardback) | ISBN 9781509538256 (pbk.)
Subjects: LCSH: Social problems. | Social interaction. | Sociology.
Classification: LCC HN18.3 (ebook) | LCC HN18.3 .A614 2019 (print) | DDC 155.4/182--dc23
LC record available at https://lccn.loc.gov/2019004021

Typeset in 10.5pt on 12pt Sabon LT Pro
by Fakenham Prepress Solutions, Fakenham, Norfolk NR21 8NL
Printed and bound in Great Britain by CPI Group (UK) Ltd, Croydon

The publisher has used its best endeavours to ensure that the URLs for external websites referred to in this book are correct and active at the time of going to press. However, the publisher has no responsibility for the websites and can make no guarantee that a site will remain live or that the content is or will remain appropriate.

Every effort has been made to trace all copyright holders, but if any have been overlooked the publisher will be pleased to include any necessary credits in any subsequent reprint or edition.

For further information on Polity, visit our website: politybooks.com

# What Makes a Social Crisis?

# Contents

# Preface and Acknowledgments

After publishing *The Civil Sphere* in 2006, I had a strong feeling that the theory could shed new light on contemporary social crises, and not only on the spreading out of historical processes of civil repair to which I had devoted Parts III and IV of that book – the social and cultural movements that challenged African–American oppression, gender inequality, and anti-Semitism over the longue durée. To that end, in 2012 I was busy clipping newspaper articles and taking notes when Trevor Stack asked me to present something at the conference "What Civil, What Society?" at the Centre for Citizenship, Civil Society and Rule of Law (CISRUL), which he directs at the University of Aberdeen. I took that opportunity to begin developing the model of societalization that is the subject of this book. The theory has developed in fits and starts, in the years between then and now, benefitting immensely from collegial criticisms and suggestions during presentations at many departmental colloquia and conferences around the world. Toward the end of this process, as I prepared a partial and condensed version for publication in the *American Sociological Review* (2018), I had the opportunity to further revise my argument in response to suggestions from the journal's anonymous reviewers and from Omar Lizardo, a co-editor. I am grateful to the *American Sociological Review* for permission to reprint material from that earlier publication.

Four Yale doctoral students – Anne Marie Champagne, Jeffrey Sachs, Sorcha Alexandrina Brophy, and Todd Madigan – provided inspired research for the empirical chapters of this book. Nadine Amalfi provided expert editorial assistance. Yale University provided sabbatical leave and research funding, and the Center for Cultural Sociology provided a congenial and stimulating intellectual atmosphere.

Being in a crisis is being at the center
Because when everything is on the line,
Everything is vital.
That is all that exists.

Karl Ove Knausgaard, *My Struggle*, Book 6

# Introduction

## Societalization in Society

Early in June 2012, in a featured op-ed in the *New York Times*, one of Germany's most influential economists opposed bailing out Greece and other ailing European economies, declaring "it doesn't make economic sense" (*New York Times* 6/13/12). In doing so, Hans-Werner Sinn reiterated an archetypal position about the proper relationship between the civil sphere and its boundaries. "Such [bailout] schemes violate the liability principle," Sinn explained, "one of the constituting principles of a market economy, which holds that it is the creditors' responsibility to choose their debtors." According to such a principle, "if debtors cannot repay, creditors should bear the losses." For states to backstop reckless creditors, for debtors who cannot repay, gravely threatens economic logic: "If we give up the liability principle, the European market economy will lose its most important allocative virtue: the careful selection of investment opportunities by creditors. We would then waste part of the capital generated by the arduous savings of earlier generations."

Sinn's argument can be viewed ideologically, as a conservative intervention in the ongoing euro crisis; it can also be viewed analytically, as an unapologetic statement about how a modern society would work if it were to be organized upon market principles alone. There is, after all, a compelling logic that defines capitalist economic systems. Only if investors and lenders are economically rational about distributing scarce resources can capital be allocated efficiently and productively. To help ensure this outcome, markets must not only threaten but actually punish investors who lack prudence. If bad investors do not lose money, then scarce time and energy is wasted. When taking on debt, creditors must carefully calculate future productive possibilities. If they are wrong, if their economic judgment is faulty, then they are punished. How else can the stringent yet economically productive rules of capitalism be maintained?

My interest here is not to challenge this argument from an economic point of view. The marketplace is vastly significant, and capitalist logic can be spectacularly effective in strictly economic terms. But the marketplace does not exhaust modern society, which is filled with places and positions that operate according to fundamentally different logics (Polanyi 1944, Friedland and Robertson 1990, Somers 2008). Sinn concluded his peroration on behalf of market society with a sarcastic reference to US President Barack Obama: "I am surprised that the president of the world's most successful capitalist nation would overlook this [*sc.* the liability principle]." But he should not have been. The United States is not just capitalist; it aspires to be also civil and democratic. If Barack Obama urged EU financial support for Greece and other ailing European economies, he did so for the same reason he had earlier advocated state support for American banks, creditors, and debtors alike. Elected to represent the civil sphere (Alexander 2010, Alexander and Jaworsky 2014), the president felt compelled to make the American state responsive to the human suffering of citizens, regardless (within limits) of economic cost. Yes, creditors and debtors had been remarkably irresponsible as economic actors, but as members of the civil sphere they deserved to be treated not only according to the logic of the market but also as human beings.

How such multiple social logics are both in tension and intertwined is my concern in this book. I theorize eruptions in the boundaries between civil and non-civil spheres and illustrate this model with reference to recent social crises around religion, economics, journalism, and gender – the pedophile crisis in the American Catholic Church commencing in 2002, the 2008 financial crisis in the United States, the UK phone hacking scandal that mushroomed in 2010, and the #MeToo crisis that began in October 2017 and continues to this day. My central question is this: How do endemic, ongoing institutional strains suddenly burst their sphere-specific boundaries and become explosive scandals in society at large? My answer begins from the premise that social problems do not, in themselves, create such broad eruptions. I argue that even severe institutional strains are typically handled by intrainstitutional authorities in ways that make such strains relatively invisible and untroubling to those on the outside. Problems become crises, I suggest, only when they move outside their own spheres and appear to endanger society at large. I call this sense of broader endangerment, and the responses it engenders, "societalization." Societalization occurs when the discourses and material resources of the civil sphere are brought into play. It is only when sphere-specific problems become *societalized* that routine strains are carefully scrutinized, once lauded institutions ferociously criticized, elites threatened and punished, and far-reaching institutional reforms launched – and sometimes made.

The first chapters in this book are devoted to the theory of societalization, addressing as they do the questions of *what*, *how*, *why*, and *why not* in a conceptual way. In chapter 1 I ask what societalization is and how it happens and I propose a sequential model, Time 1 ($T_1$) to Time 5 ($T_5$). In chapter 2 I look at the agents that push societalization through this temporal sequence. In chapter 3 I engage the null hypothesis ("why not?"), conceptualizing why societalization often does not happen when it seems that it would or should, and I outline limit conditions. In the later chapters I present four case studies that empirically elaborate upon and develop the model. These discussions are based on primary sources and represent new, empirical-cum-theoretical takes on crises that, with the exception of #MeToo, have been written about many times before. In conclusion I ask why societalization has not been explained before; and I address it not as a problem in society but as a problem of social theory.

The ambition of this essay is theoretical. I aim here to introduce a new macro-sociological model of structure and process. Macro, because it addresses society as a whole; structural, because it focuses on long-established, deeply institutionalized social spheres; process, because it details a dynamic sequence of conflict and struggle between competing material and ideal interests in distinctive societal domains. I believe that this theoretical aim can be advanced, however, only to the degree that I imbed my conceptual claims in dense and detailed case studies.[1] Theory is abstract; it must also be made concrete. A new theory must be "seen," and perhaps even "felt" and "experienced," for its plausibility to be entertained. It must become familiar before it can subject itself to more rigorous testing.

# 1

# What Is Societalization and How Does It Happen?

The civil sphere is a real social force, but it is also an idealized community, one that is imagined as being composed of individuals who are autonomous yet mutually obligated, who experience solidarity even as they respect one another's independence (Alexander 2006, Kivisto and Sciortino 2015, Alexander and Tognato 2018, Alexander, Stack, and Khoshrokovar 2019, Alexander, Palmer, Park, and Ku 2019, Alexander, Lund, and Voyer 2019). In cultural terms, the civil sphere is organized around a discourse that sacralizes the motives, relations, and institutions necessary to sustain democratic forms of self-regulation and social solidarity. This involves qualities such as honesty, rationality, openness, independence, cooperation, participation, and equality (Jacobs 1996, 2000, Mast 2006, 2012, Smith 1991, 2005, Kivisto and Sciortino 2015). The discourse of civil society is binary: it also identifies and pollutes qualities that endanger democracy, such as deceit, hysteria, dependence, secrecy, aggression, hierarchy, and inequality.[1] The civil sphere, moreover, is not only discursive. It possesses a powerful materiality. Communicative institutions such as factual and fictional mass media, public opinion polls, and civil associations provide the organizational capacity to specify broad discursive categories in time and place. They purify some events, institutions, and groups as civil and good, rewarding them with recognition; they pollute others as dangerously anti-civil, humiliating them as evil. The civil sphere sustains powerful regulative institutions as well: the complex apparatuses of law, office, and elections apply sanctions that are backed through state coercion and make cultural evaluations stick. Those who are deemed civil are rewarded not only with prestige but with political power; those constructed as anti-civil are not simply disrespected but threatened, arrested, rendered bankrupt, and sometimes made to suffer physical harm.

Vis-à-vis other, *non*-civil institutional-cum-cultural fields, the civil sphere is at once oppositional and aspirational, which means that interinstitutional boundaries are never settled, never set in concrete. Because civil institutions project communicative interpretations and apply regulative sanctions in real time and space, nothing about the location and traction of civil boundaries is certain; they cannot be ascertained in the abstract (Ku 1998). What is deemed to be civil? What is deemed not to be? These questions have been answered in remarkably disparate ways over the course of historical time, the answers determining where boundaries between the civil sphere and other, non-civil spheres of social life are laid. Should gender hierarchy be considered a family affair, handled by the domestic sphere's patriarchal elites, or should it be seen as violating broader, more civil norms, such that intrafamily domination and violence become scandalous to society at large (Alexander 2001, Luengo 2018)? Should what goes on inside churches stay within these houses of worship, as a matter between believers and their god, or should the dispensation of God's grace be subject to civil scrutiny? Should a productive but also exploitative and unstable capitalist economy be left alone, to work its markets for better and for worse, or should more solidaristic and civil considerations intervene (Lee 2018, Ngai and Ng 2019, Olave 2018)? Should news reporters be free to roam for information as they may, intruding when, where, and how they see fit, or should they be subject to legal and moral constraints? Modern civil spheres have continually legitimated what later, down the line, came to be seen as egregiously anti-civil practices (Alexander 1988). A practice that seems acceptable at one point can become deeply offensive at another. Forms of religion, sexuality, politics, and economic life that once appeared to facilitate civil society are later reconstructed as dangerously destructive intrusions whose very existence undermines civil motives and relations.

Blumer (1971: 302) once observed that "the pages of history are replete with dire conditions unnoticed and unattended to." Yet, while real existing civil spheres are deeply compromised, they are also endemically restless, creating fertile opportunities for calling out the very injustices they legitimate. It is because the utopian promises of civil spheres are never fully institutionalized that these promises continuously trigger radical criticism, social movement struggles, social crises, and institutional reform.

My aim is to conceptualize the relative, labile, shifting status of social problems, not in historical or interactional but in analytic terms – as a systemic, macro-sociological process. One might imagine, at time $T_1$, a hypothetical "steady state" of boundary relations between civil and non-civil spheres, in which there *appears* to be empirical stability and there is *imagined* to be reciprocity between spheres. In a putatively steady state of this sort, most members of the civil sphere do not experience the operations of other spheres as destructive intrusions and do not abrogate existing institutional boundaries to mount antagonistic efforts at repairing the insides of another sphere.[2] There is no doubt, of course, that every social sphere experiences continuous, often severe strains. In the economy, there are irresponsible decisions and underserved losses, bankruptcies and thefts, inflations and recessions. The religious world experiences continual financial corruption, wrenching disciplinary and recruiting failures, and polarizing theological disputes. In the world of journalism, the boundaries of privacy and publicity are continuously challenged, professional norms are cast aside, plagiarism is frequent, and media elites often conflate financial self-interest with professional responsibility. The intimate sphere of sexual relations is rife with frustration, misunderstanding, bruised feelings, and worse – and these do not cease when they enter the occupational domain.

In conditions of steady state, however, such strains are institutionally insulated; because they remain intrasphere, they do not generate significant attention outside. Failing to arouse the concern of extrainstitutional outsiders, strains are addressed in non-civil ways. Indeed, subject to intrasphere logics (Friedland and Alford 1991), strains often bolster rather than challenge organizational authority. Rather than degrading civil sphere ideals, strains in the steady state may actually appear to confirm institutional and cultural pluralism.

But steady state breaks down with societalization, transforming a heretofore routinely accepted practice into a new social fact (Durkheim 1966 [1895]), one that seems evil and symbolically profane. A practice that once aroused little interest outside a particular institution now appears threatening to "society" itself. What was once normal comes to be viewed as pathological, as morally polluted and socially disruptive. It becomes what Mary Douglas (1966) called "matter out of place": something dirty and polluted in response to which strenuous efforts at purification must be made (Cottle 2004, 2011).

Societalization begins at time $T_2$, when a semiotic code (see Tavory and Swidler 2009) is triggered, moving public attention space (Hilgartner and Bosk 1988) from institutional part to civil whole. When social language switches in such a manner, critical and emancipatory narratives arise and vast material resources can be brought into play. When journalism interprets intrainstitutional strains as violations of the civil sphere, ordinary occurrences can be converted into events (Mast 2006, 2012, Sewell 1996, Wagner-Pacifici 2010, 2017). Event-ness announces the breakdown of steady state. Outrage arouses the "conscience of society," confidence and trust give way to fear and alarm. Harsh regulatory interventions often follow (time $T_3$), for civil communicative and regulatory institutions are intertwined. However, in response to such new cultural judgments and regulatory interventions, backlash builds up (time $T_4$). Thrown on the defensive, the targeted institutions and elites attack the newly intrusive civil sphere and its carrier groups. Intersphere boundaries – where to draw the lines between spheres – now become objects of intense and bitter struggle. There is a war between spheres. It is such a situation of standoff, as much as the achievement of civil repair, that creates the almost inevitable pathway back to steady state (time $T_5$).

Social strains are real; they have material consequences, and sometimes, as in economic crisis or war, such consequences can be very harsh indeed. Nonetheless, it is not the substance of strain that causes societalization, but rather how such strains are understood. This is a matter for societal interpretation – namely of what a strain is, why it happened, who was responsible for creating it, and whom it hurts. Answering these questions determines how strains are perceived and what can be done to keep them from happening again (Alexander, Eyerman, Giesen, and Smelser 2004).

When semiotic shifts push social problems beyond steady state, the moral and institutional foundations of society itself seem endangered, and there are fears that the center will not hold (Shils 1975). These broad anxieties typically become focused on the civil institution of office, a key regulative institution of the civil sphere (Alexander 2006: 132–50). Office translates idealizing discourse about moral solidarity into the institutional requirement that leadership should be responsible and other-oriented, demanding that power eschew nepotism and self-dealing. At the heart of a democratic society is the fervent belief – the conceit, a cynic might say – that power not only should, but can, be exercised in a manner that will serve the public good and that the civil institution of office should, and can, be occupied by goodwilled human beings. To the degree that civil spheres have teeth, those who possess power are bound by a vocation, a calling in Weber's sense, to the ethics of office (Weber 1927 [1904–5]). When semiotic shifts define a strain as endangering the civil center, institutional authorities are accused of having abrogated their official responsibilities; they are attacked as unworthy and unfit; strenuous efforts are made to remove them from office; and significant repairs can be made to institutional norms and structures.

At $T_1$, the communicative and regulative institutions of the civil sphere defer to the mores and interests of intrainstitutional elites. At $T_2$, such civil hands-off-ness is reinterpreted, retroactively, as a dereliction of civil responsibility, as a cover-up that has prevented polluted practices from being subject to the moral commitments of the civil sphere. At $T_3$, those who possess civil power respond to this dereliction in a material manner, issuing threats and sanctions. At $T_4$, the challenged institutional elites fight back. A war between the spheres ensues, one that eventually compels carrier groups that represent the civil sphere to abandon their avenging quest. The separation between spheres is reconstructed, and with it an ambivalent, ambiguous, and contested return to steady state ($T_5$). Once an overwhelming social crisis, the initial trigger is now seen in the rearview mirror through societalization. It becomes an historic "episode," narrated in legend and myth, remembered in anniversaries, and performatively inscribed in cinema and television.[3] Yet the strains that had once energized it do not entirely disappear. Instead they are recontextualized, becoming, once again, matters of primarily intrainstitutional concern. While abuses occasionally are publicly noted as worrisome occurrences that violate contemporary norms, they are not constructed as earthshaking events. Fears for the center are no longer triggered, and there is a reassuring recognition that, after societalization, new organizational structures are in place. That these repairs may not entirely blunt old strains and that, even if they do, new strains reflecting boundary tension are bound to emerge – these are not worries in the steady state.

# 2

# Who Are the Agents of Societalization?

Why does the social process called societalization occur? How is it possible that a temporal sequence can unfold in response to critical interpretations of strains, such that steady states are undermined, crises mushroom, and civil repairs become possible, before backlashes emerge and boundaries between spheres rebuild?

At the most general level, the reason is social differentiation. It is the cultural and organizational separation of social spheres that allows societalization, the fundamental incompatibility between functional requisites and their spheres of justice (Walzer 1984) – not the reciprocity and complementarity of differentiated structures and functions, as is so commonly alleged. But, beyond the fact of agonistic spheres, a relatively autonomous civil sphere – the sphere of societal justice, at once cultural and organizational, so rarely conceptualized by differentiation theory (see the Conclusion of this book) – is the "mechanism" (Gross 2009, Norton 2014b) at the heart of the machine. It supplies the binary discourse that allows for actions to be inspired and degraded, fuels the institutions that bristle at one another's prerogatives, and peoples the elites whose ideal and material interests, prickly to begin with, can be so abraded as to seem inimical in the extreme.

But who actually carries the water? Who evokes the discourse? Whose institutional prerogatives feel raw and bristled? In short, what sorts of people and roles make up the civil sphere's elites?

There are occupational groups that carry in their bones the ideal interests of the civil sphere. Realizing these interests is what they live and die for; it marks the be all and end all of their careers, the culminating moments of their lives. They are the agents of societalization. Societalization is not only about systems, spheres, and institutions. It is also about social actors and the meanings they give to their activities, and others'. The communicative and regulative institutions of the civil sphere don't act by themselves; they are energized by people whose ideal interests compel them to societalize, and whose material status is enhanced if they succeed. Journalists and prosecutors eagerly ferret out and punish what they interpret as civil violations. They are investigative reporters, editors, and publishers; crusading lawyers, district attorneys, attorneys general, and judges. They see potentially anti-civil actions everywhere; they feel personally enraged at them; and, in their professional capacities, they engage in activities aimed at arousing others to feel civil outrage as well. Finding "holy shit stories" (Havill 1993: 68) and "red hot cases" (Samuelsohn 2017) is what they're all about, why they got into the game.

At the microlevel, societalization can be conceptualized as a series of performances and counterperformances (Alexander 2011, Alexander, Giesen, and Mast 2006, Mast 2006, Norton 2014a, Reed 2013) by highly interested and motivated parties. Investigative journalists scan the social horizon for big stories, seeing themselves as guardians at the gate. Weaving incriminating narratives out of seemingly separate facts, journalists launch critical interpretations to publics who may read, listen, and view, hoping against hope that these citizen audiences will fuse with their indignant narrations, sharing their rage. Editors place what they judge to be seriously egregious reports about civil calumny on the front page, at the top of the hour, at the beginning of the digital news feed. Publishers supply critical resources for reporters and editors and then watch their behinds. Prosecutors circle like birds of prey, looking down with hawk eyes, itching to come in for the kill. When instructed by news stories and emboldened by public outrage, irate prosecutors charge ahead. Commanding new resources from anxious politicians and alienated state officials, they oversee special investigators who look for examples of malfeasance, issue arrest warrants, and organize evidence and precedence that allow charges to stand up in court. They sequester grand juries, issue damning reports, and demand harsh penalties. If these activities succeed, there is not only a deep sense of personal vindication but social glory. Fame, stardom, prizes, and higher office await.

Audiences are primed to be receptive to such civil performances by virtue of their belief in the discourse of civil society, that it is sacred and that its ideals should be protected from harm. Such background belief is necessary, but it is not sufficient. Only if these general codes have been organized into established "scandal genres" will contemporary reports of civil crimes be credible and moral and emotional significance assigned. If pedophilia has already been powerfully scandalized, if financial crises have repeatedly been notorious, if yellow journalism has long been criticized and feared, if sexism and harassment have been identified and polluted, they form scandal genres that provide background representations against which contemporary performances of civil indignation can arouse indignation, metalanguages about scandal that allow pragmatic speech acts about new scandalous actions to be felicitous (Austin 1957), to succeed performatively. In steady state, the background stories that constitute scandal genres lay latent; they are triggered by skilled performers who wring from them action-specific scripts about the civil horrors of the present day. If code-switching scripts are compelling, if the other elements of social performance are available, and if the social stars are aligned, the performance of scandal will fuse with audiences (Alexander 2011) and civil repair will proceed, until backlash intervenes.[1]

When their performances of civil indignation succeed, journalists and prosecutors become not merely agents but heroes.[2] For the wider citizenry, they become legendary, larger-than-life figures whose daring deeds exemplify truth, justice, and – in the United States – the American way (Bradlee 1995: 384). For the members of their occupations, they become sacred icons of exemplary professional practice (ibid., 369; Revers 2017). After Watergate, Bob Woodward and Carl Bernstein were the new "all-American folk heroes," as *Washington Post* Editor Ben Bradlee attested in his memoirs, "profiled in magazine after magazine, giving speeches all over the country" (Bradlee 1995: 384); and Bradlee emphasizes that they became "cult heroes in the annals of journalism" as well (ibid., 369). Recounting the rise to glory of civil heroes, biographers become hagiographers who tell a story of David and Goliath. Two decades after Watergate, after noting that 200 books had already been written on the topic, Adrian Havill offered a rationale for his own *Lives of Bob Woodward and Carl Bernstein* right out of folklore: "What has always fascinated most observers was how two – albeit talented and tenacious – young reporters were, seemingly alone, able to unravel the entire labyrinthine scheme of political sabotage, defamatory acts, income tax fraud, and ... obstructions of justice by the administration of Richard Nixon" (Havill 1993: 72). The young reporters not only were seen by others but saw themselves, too, as giant killers. A friend recollected Bernstein's response, in Watergate's early days, to an out-of-town weekend invitation: "I can't come up this weekend because I'm working on a story that can bring down the President" (ibid., 75). Such heroic narratives about civil salvation emerge in particular historical situations, but they have an independent, structural status (Barthes 1977). In describing his occupation, the legendary left-wing journalist I. F. Stone evoked sacrality and holy war, telling an interviewer that "being a newspaperman has always seemed a cross between Galahad and William Randolph Hearst, a perpetual crusade" (Stone 1963).

Civil heroes view their work less as a job than a vocation. In her Pulitzer Prize-winning autobiography *Personal History*, Katherine Graham, the *Washington Post* publisher about whom elegiac films continue to be made, called journalism a "mission" (Graham 1997: 434); in his Preface to *Reporters Who Made History*, Steven Hallock called it a "passion" and a "noble calling" (Hallock 2010: xvi). Employing the same Protestant analogy, so central to Max Weber's (1927 [1904–5]) theory about the cultural basis of modern responsibility, Woodward's biographer traced the reporter's *Bildung* (formation) to the "straight arrow Calvinist culture of Wheaton [College's] self-righteous ideals" (Havill 1993: 7). Morris Dees, the co-founder of the Southern Poverty Law Center, who made his name as a legendary advocate for civil rights, declares there is "no higher calling" (Dees 2011: 347) than lawyering, claiming that "trial lawyers hold the keys to the gates of justice" (ibid., 348) and rhapsodizing that, when their legal victories open up these gates, lawyers experience "a higher justice, a love we speak so much of but know so little about" (ibid., 334). Prosecutors and journalists speak insistently about personal obligation and moral responsibility. Writing about her newspaper's role in the Pentagon Papers crisis, Graham attested that "we regarded their publication not as a breach of national security ... but as a contribution to the national interest, indeed as the obligation of a respectable newspaper" (Graham 1997: 457). It is not about making money but about "the journalist's yearning to make a difference," Dan Rather asserted (Friend 2015: 30). Ben Bradlee recalled that, after returning from World War II, "it was hard for me to enjoy doing nothing." While a family friend "had always wanted me to work in his brokerage office," he remembers, "I was sure I wanted to do something that would make the world a better place, that would really make a difference" (Bradlee 1995: 94).

Civil heroes see themselves not as committed to some particular ideology or policy position, but as the vessels of a transcendent morality, one defined by a binary set of truth, openness, and reason, on one side, and deception, secrecy, and irrationality, on the other. The pioneering muckraker Upton Sinclair serialized his exposé of the meatpacking industry in *Appeal to Reason*, a progressive-era, socialist magazine. Robert Redford entitled his earnest documentary about the CBS journalist Dan Rather *Truth* (Friend 2015). Richard Ben-Veniste, the crusading prosecutor who got his start during the Watergate investigation, entitled his autobiography *The Emperor's New Clothes: Exposing the Truth from Watergate to 9/11*. "If somebody sets out to lie, you're dead," Ben Bradlee explained to celebrity interviewer David Frost, adding: "Walt Lippman said it all in 1910[:] To make the truth emerge, you don't have to get it right the first time. You get a small bit [and] it takes years" (Bradlee 1991). His scion Ben Bradlee, Jr., editor of the *Boston Globe* during the

"Spotlight" investigation of church pedophilia, wrote that "the story began, as all do, with a group of reporters trying to answer a set of questions," and "then escalated as they discovered how church officials kept the ugly truth under wraps" (Bradlee 2002: x). For Katherine Graham, journalism aimed "to open up the system and expose its workings" (Graham 1997: 457).

It is their commitment to moral universalism that allows civil heroes to defend independence against the hierarchical, anti-civil powers that be, against the rich and powerful whom they portray as preying upon virtuous citizens. The celebrated progressive-era defense attorney Clarence Darrow avowed: "I have lived my life and I have fought my battles, not against the weak and poor – but against power, injustice, [and] against oppression" (Darrow 1961: 497). Charles Edward Russell, another muckraking progressive-era journalist, famously belittled the US Senate as "a chamber of butlers for industrialists and financiers" (Russell 1933: 143). Describing his position as FBI director, James Comey explained, "the term is 10 years to ensure independence," so that "power does not come to be concentrated in one person and unconstrained," so that "abuse of power" is avoided (Comey 2013). Eric McLeish, leading prosecutor of Boston pedophile priests, recalls: "I became a lawyer because I don't like bullies and I don't like bullies who are in a position of power" (Henderson 2016). Ben-Veniste proclaims: "I don't like being lied to. Never have. Over a long career as a lawyer, I have sometimes had the opportunity to do something about it. Exposing the hypocrisy and mendacity of officials in positions of power has held a special appeal for me" (Ben-Veniste 2009: 2). John Keker, a top prosecutor in the Iran–Contra Affair, identifies himself as "on the side of the beleaguered and attacked rather than the behemoth," declaring his "love of being against the government [and] the smug and sanctimonious" and acknowledging the "fun" he has "punctur[ing] the balloon of pomp and smugness" (Beeson 2015). Dan Rather describes his journalistic career as "trying to uncover stuff that would send people to the fire pits" (Friend 2015). Reviewing the film *Spotlight*, which follows the eponymous investigation, the *Atlantic* lauds the *Boston Globe* for not being "beholden to moneyed interests" and for having the "will to push past any political or social pressure" (Scott 2015). In *Henry VI*, Shakespeare poeticized: "if tyranny is to prevail, we must first kill all the lawyers." Morris Dees assures his readers: "we still face tyrants. Tire manufacturers knowingly allow defective tires to remain on the road. Tobacco companies kill thousands each year ... while hiding damaging medical fact. Financial institutions and credit card companies defraud the poor [and] small used-car dealers knowingly sell defective autos ... The victims of these modern-day tyrants desperately need courageous lawyers. Representing them [gives] real meaning to our professional lives, building up rewards and treasures far more important than the money we take to the bank" (Dees 2011: 346). Katherine Graham puts it most simply: she describes "rulers and reporters" as "natural antagonists" (Graham 1997: 457).

The anti-authoritarian assaults in which civil heroes engage are portrayed not as self-serving and vainglorious adventures, but as courageous sacrifices on behalf of the people, the members of the civil sphere to whom power is made accountable via the regulation of office. "Anything a public official does wrong," observed the journalist turned public broadcasting guru Alistair Cooke shortly after the publication of Woodward and Bernstein's *All the President's Men*, "will end up on the front page" (Havill 1993: xix). The *New York Times* praised the film *Spotlight* for "confront[ing] evil without sensationalism," the evil being "the way power operates in the absence of accountability" (Scott 2015). In his book on the progressive era, the historian Richard Hofstader elides the occupation of journalist with civil repair, writing: "the Progressive mind was characteristically a journalistic mind" – that of "the socially responsible reporter-reformer" (Hofstader 1955: 186).

If disinterest and self-abnegation characterize the moral ethic of civil heroes (see Revers 2017: 43–78), it hardly describes their emotions, which seethe with spluttering outrage and distemper. Robert Redford calls Dan Rather a "savage," and the journalist himself acknowledges "I burn with a hot, hard flame," describing "justice [as] the red beating heart of democracy" (Friend 2015). Clinton Bamberger gave off a "fire for justice," one colleague affirmed about the defense lawyer who championed impoverished defendants and established the "Brady rule" expanding defendant rights (Roberts 2017). Keker became involved in the Oliver North case because he was "outraged" by revelations of a covert war in Central America. "I hated the war in Vietnam," he said. "And I thought it was an outrage that some macho people were making war in an unauthorized way in Central America" (Guthrie 2014). David Halberstam's reporting from Vietnam was so "inflammatory," eulogized the *Washington Post*, that President Kennedy pleaded with "the publisher of the *New York Times* [to] remove him from the war beat" (Allen 2007). Temper and outrage generate courage and tenacity in the face of anti-civil danger. "Blazingly Bright, Fearlessly Focused" is how the *Wall Street Journal* headlined its review of *Spotlight* (Morgenstern 2015). "She was one of the most tenacious – almost ferocious – reporters I have ever worked with," testified a colleague about a Pulitzer Prize-winning reporter whose work exposed scientology (Meacham 2011), adding: "every cliché, including the one about the bulldog that gets a hold of an ankle and won't let go, was true of her" (ibid.). When Robert Mueller was named director of the FBI, a former Department of Justice spokesperson called him an "inspired choice," attesting: "As a fraud and foreign bribery expert, he knows how to follow the money. Who knows what they will find, but if there is something to be found, he will find it" (Lewis 2001).

When prosecutors find the evidence for fraud and bribery, however, they can't always make it stick, and when tenacious reporters and intrepid editors publish outraged exposés, these don't always inflame. In *Death of a Salesman*, when Linda Loman decries her husband Willy's tragic life, she exclaims: "attention must be paid." But often it is not. Stories about civil abuse don't stick, lawsuits don't convict. Performances of civil outrage don't fuse with the citizen audience. Scandal is performed but audiences do not exclaim. Despite "the press investigat[ing] Iran–Contra to a fare-thee-well," Ben Bradlee remembered, it "still never managed to engage the nation's attention or conscience. The public's throat was never seized by Iran–Contra as it had been seized by Watergate" (Bradlee 1995: 409).

All this points to limit conditions.

# 3

# Why Does Societalization NOT Happen?

The civil sphere is restless and imperious. As it is surrounded by non-civil institutions whose ideas of justice can often seem anti-civil, there are innumerable boundary issues that can, in principle, stir the civil sphere up. When civil heroes put their shoulders to the wheel, the booming voice of the civil sphere can be heard above others and its powerful regulatory institutions can hold sway. In such moments, objects of civil indignation can be humiliated and punished, and the moral bonds that structure civil office can be revivified. Repairs can be made to institutional structures, reworking the incentives and sanctions that shape organization and revising the occupational cultures that establish prestige and sustain authoritative power.

In societalization as an ideal type, a sequence of civil repair stretches from strain inside steady state to code switch, regulative reconstruction, backlash, and return to steady state. The case studies I undertake below illustrate this model empirically. Each triggered the same causal sequence, and, with the exception of #MeToo, each societalizating episode was complete.

Such fully enunciated sequences of societalization are, however, more the exception than the rule. Significant institutional strains often do not trigger societalization. Code switching from intrainstitutional to civil criteria often seems utopian in the extreme. Moreover, even when societalization is triggered, it often stalls. Even when it does not stall, societalization can lead to spiraling conflicts that undermine the civil sphere rather than repairing it.

History is replete with grave episodes when societies have not been able to sustain moral outrage, when regulatory institutions have failed to act, and when badly needed civil repairs have not been made. In the early and mid-nineteenth century, there was great financial malfeasance and crushing economic setback, but societal-wide crises rarely ensued. Only as labor and middle-class reform movements gained recognition did economic crises begin to have broader civil repercussions, and the devastation of the laboring classes come increasingly to be experienced as damaging to the social whole (Polanyi 1944). Gender bias, sexual harassment, and violence against women by men inside modern institutional arenas – family, school, and workplace – transpired unabated for centuries, considered hardly worth mentioning. When they did surface, they were usually treated as kerfuffles and handled intrainstitutionally by the patriarchal powers that be (Kerber and De Hart 1995). Only in the last half-century did such abuses begin to generate code switching and societalization, an episodic process that continues to erupt today. Or consider harassment and police violence against racial minorities. Despite the victory of abolitionism, it took 75 years after the North's victory in the American Civil War – until the middle of the New Deal – for the lynching of African Americans to become societalized (Zangrando 1980). And systemic police killing of black men continues up to the present day. Code switching and regulatory intervention have recently been triggered in response to such anti-civil depredations, but civil repairs have so far only haltingly been made (Ostertag 2019).

Such examples of blocked and stalled societalization point to two categories of conditions that limit the ideal-typical model presented here. These are marginalization and polarization.

## Marginalization

Societalization is blocked or stalled insofar as those subject to institutional strain and dysfunction are subaltern groups

(Fraser 1992). When stigmatized populations are hived off into segregated institutions and communities, the strains they are subjected to and the social techniques they have devised for addressing them are invisible to, or ignored by, those whose perceptions are mediated by the communicative institutions of the dominant civil sphere and whose actions are regulated thereby.

This was certainly the case for the predations that manual workers suffered in early industrial capitalism (Marshall 1965); for Jews in medieval and early modern European societies (Trachtenberg 1961); for colonized peoples under imperialism (Said 1978); for South African blacks under apartheid rule (Frederickson 1981); for African Americans subject to slavery, Jim Crow, and northern ghettoization (ibid.); for Irish Catholics in Northern Ireland after the end of the civil war and before the Good Friday agreements (Kane 2019); for women in patriarchal societies (Pateman 1988); and for gay and lesbians in hetero-normative ones (Seidman 1992). The strains and impositions to which such marginalized groups were subject were unlikely to be reported in mainstream media; and even when such reports did appear, they would rarely generate code switching (Jacobs 2000). Between center and periphery, there was little sense of common humanity, thus less chance for shared cognition and emotional feeling. Core groups imagine such peripheral persons as less than fully human, as lacking civil capacity (Landes 1988). To protect themselves from pollution by these putatively dangerous others, central groups engage in hostile aggression rather than in empathic societalization, withdrawing to privileged enclaves rather than reaching out to underprivileged communities (Massey and Denton 1993).

In the face of such deeply rooted blockages to societalization, other kinds of responses to strain may arise, responses that provide decidedly less direct pathways to amelioration. Social movements can emerge, some moderate, others more radical, confronting rigid hierarchies and projecting felicitous performances of injustice (Eyerman 2006, Eyerman and Jamison 1991, Kane 2019, Ostertag 2019). Intellectuals can make scathing critiques, and social scientists launch far-reaching investigations; white papers can be published, and religious jeremiads made (Smith and Howe 2015).

Such social-cum-cultural reactions to blocked societalization appeal to an idealized civil sphere, free from the destructive compromises that have created marginalization in the actually existing, "real" civil societies of the day. If such protests gain traction, they affect the asymmetrical background of cultural representations against which subaltern institutional strains are viewed and excused. Indignant, counterhegemonic narratives emerge about abusive, anti-civil domination, and these new understandings are deposited in the broader collective consciousness (Branch 1988, Cott 1987, Pfohl 1977).[1] There is the gradual accretion of melodramatic stories about the pathos of sexual abuse, pedophilia, financial corruption, and reckless and irresponsible journalism. These are interwoven stories about new civil heroes, romantic narratives about courageous individuals and movements that resisted anti-civil forces and institutions – and sometimes triumphed.[2]

Building up such a reservoir of sacred and profane background representations is a necessary – if not sufficient – condition for the processes of societalization I have described below. Financial corruption and the selfish greed of economic elites have been staples of American popular culture for almost two centuries; such schemas are easily evoked by events that trigger societalization. Stories about power-hungry media barons and ruthless reporters are also long-standing popular narratives that provide a potent background for institutional events to arouse civil indignation. Priestly pedophilia, by contrast, has been more of an underground narrative in western societies (Jenkins 1996), but in the last three decades of the twentieth century (Pfohl 1977) the practice of pedophilia more broadly came under increasingly intense scrutiny as a dangerous practice to which civil spheres must attend. This heightened pollution provided a vivid background for institutional reports on intrachurch practices. Feminist challenges to male power had long supplied wrenching, melodramatic stories of perfidious male domination; representations of sexism as a male trait and of sexual harassment as a male activity were recent accretions to the counternarratives that provided the background for "MeToo" societalization.

## Polarization

If societies are sharply divided against themselves, however, this growing recognition of anti-civil abuse is not enough. Social indignation can become refracted in a manner that fails to engage the full horizon of common concern. The paradoxical result is that societalization, rather than expanding solidarity, actually intensifies division, and such deepening division can lead to the weakening, and sometimes even destruction, of the civil sphere rather than to its strengthening and repair.

Consider the enslavement of African Americans in the antebellum United States. Abolition movements created increasing sensitivity to slavery and eventually massive indignation. However, the outrage was experienced primarily among northern, not southern, whites. The former began to experience code switch, but northern media projections failed to fuse with broad audiences in the white South. Over time, those who promoted the societalization of slavery and those who blocked it came to see each other as irredeemably anti-civil, as enemies who must be physically destroyed if the northern and southern civil spheres were to be preserved. After decades of rhetorical and regulatory failure, force seemed the only way. Only after military victory were northern civil institutions able to intrude into the southern civil sphere and to begin efforts to repair it – the Reconstruction project that, after a decade, was itself rolled back (Foner 1988).

Or consider the societalization of anti-Semitism in nineteenth- and early twentieth-century Europe. For decades, Western European societies introduced civil repairs that allowed incorporation, providing Jewish people with political, economic, and cultural citizenship. This societalizing dynamic, however, eventually created extraordinary blowback, deepening chasms opening up between more cosmopolitan and more primordial cultural and political forces and elites. In France, after Jewish incorporation had proceeded apace throughout much of the nineteenth century, the Dreyfus affair exploded in the 1890s. Public expression of anti-Semitic sentiment dramatically increased, deepening political and cultural polarization and setting the stage for Vichy's collaboration with Nazi occupation four decades later (Griffiths 1991, Marrus and Paxton 1981). In Germany, Jews had been even more rapidly incorporated than in France. Yet the backlash there was that much more brutal. With defeat in World War I and the instabilities of Weimar, the continuing societalization of anti-Semitism had the perverse effect of inflaming Jew hatred and of triggering an avalanche of viciously anti-Jewish acts. This backlash eventually destroyed the German civil sphere and, soon after, German Jewry itself.

The broad social prerequisites for initiating and sustaining societalization are reasonably clear. For democratic criticism and reform to be enacted, there must be social and cultural differentiation – institutional pluralism to challenge sectorial material power, moral universalism to transcend the particularistic moral logics of the reigning powers that be. Only under such conditions can effective organizational and cultural counterpower emerge, providing platforms for societal-wide actions that transcend the segmented status quo of steady state. However, inasmuch as differentiated societies marginalize groups, to that degree societalization will not be triggered vis-à-vis the institutional strains that have created such exclusion. Neither can processes of societalization be sustained if differentiated societies are deeply polarized, culturally and organizationally (see Rueschemeyer 1986). In other words, alongside organizational and symbolic capacities to generate intersphere conflicts, there must also be significant intertextuality (Kristeva 1980). Citizen audiences must feel, or be made to feel, that they share standards of civil evaluation even when they do not share more delimited ideological and institutional interests.

Such a shared background of cultural meaning makes it possible for coalitions of counterelites to engage in mutual exhortation and to demand that sanctioning be brought to bear. It makes it more likely that performances of civil outrage can be projected to sympathetic audiences. The binary discourse of civil society and its cautionary stories of corruption, conspiracy, greed, and abuse provide background conditions for the code switching that triggers societalization, for the creation of a script about civil outrage in this or that particular time and place. In this newly coded script, strain becomes trauma (Eyerman, Alexander, and Breese 2011).

Once admired authorities are recast as perpetrators, once honored audiences redefined as victims. The bar of justice is raised. Legendary figures from the sacred civil past infuse contemporary civil performances, and new civil heroes are made. Institutional force is leveraged, significant civil repairs are made.

# 4
# Church Pedophilia

## Steady State

Sexual relations between adult authorities and minors had taken place inside the Roman Catholic Church for centuries (O'Conaill 1995: 21, White and Terry 2008). In 2010, in his Christmas address to cardinals and other church officials, Pope Benedict XVI suggested that, as late as the 1970s, "pedophilia was theorized as something feeling in conformity with man even with children" (*Belfast Telegraph* 12/21/10). An extraordinarily revealing effort at self-exculpation, this statement betrays the sharp contrast between intrainstitutional values and the perspectives of those on the outside. While the pope earnestly declared that pedophilia was widely accepted in the church of the 1970s, the practice was sharply stigmatized in the wider society, not only during that decade but also in the one before. What began to change for the church after the 1970s was not its own view of the practice, but rather the moral and institutional environment outside. A series of scandals began to remove priestly pedophilia from inside the church and put it onto the front pages of newspapers and onto the steps of courthouses. The wall separating the civil sphere and church pedophilia was made visible and unattractive, and it was gradually undermined.

The Catholic hierarchy had never officially encouraged pedophilia. However, during the long period of steady state, the church successfully engaged in intrainstitutional efforts to keep the existence of such activities hidden from those outside its boundaries. How did Catholic religion understand pedophilia, and how did its elites respond to the practice? The brunt of churchly efforts was devoted to sustaining Catholicism's own moral evaluations and to keeping institutional responses in-house. According to the head of the Congregation of Clergy, priestly pedophilia, while regrettable, was to be regarded as "an unavoidable fact of life" (*New York Times* [*NYT*] 7/2/10). This is a plausible understanding in light of a certain reading of Christian values. Immoral behavior, rather than violating universal moral standards, seems merely to confirm the fallen nature of humankind. "Priests are flawed creatures" like the rest of us, a high church official explained (*NYT* 3/28/02). If contrition does not produce a change in attitude and behavior, the only hope, according to another church official, is to pray that "this difficult problem will be resolved" (*NYT* 4/20/02). "The transforming power of God's grace is at the heart of Christian teaching," one bishop explained; "the notion that someone is irredeemable is alien" to Catholic culture (ibid.; see also Bruni and Burkett 2002 [1993]: 167; *USA Today* 4/22/02a). From such a churchly perspective, then, priestly pedophilia does not challenge the steady state of intersphere relations. It does not merit public condemnation, much less arrest and imprisonment. What it calls for, rather, is confession and submission to intrasphere authority: "When a priest expresses sorrow, it derails the judicial process in cannon law"; for, "if he seeks Reconciliation," then "Canon law gives him absolution" (*NYT* 4/20/02).

Armed with this justification by faith, church authorities confronted the growing alarm over pedophilia by demanding deference to intrainstitutional cultural authority. Before he became Pope Benedict, Cardinal Joseph Ratzinger was deeply implicated in the church's decades-long intrainstitutional struggle to make sure that pedophilia was contained. The cardinal served as director of the Congregation for the Doctrine of the Faith, which had been granted authority over sexual abuse since 1922. In his two decades as director, however,

Cardinal Ratzinger chose never to exercise this nominal authority (*NYT* 7/2/10). "Clerical culture took precedence," the future pope's biographer explained: the cardinal had great "concern for the proper order of authority" (*NYT* 4/30/10). When the abuses first became public and the US bishops' conferences formed to confront them, Cardinal Ratzinger warned that creating policies to eliminate pedophilia has "no theological basis" and that, despite the intrachurch origins of these nascent efforts at reform, the latter "do not belong to the structure of the church" (*NYT* 6/14/02).

Alongside this kind of cultural motivation for maintaining the steady state, intrainstitutional efforts to contain pedophilia were spurred on by the practical exigencies of maintaining the church as an ongoing, functional organization. "The temptation of all churches," one religious observer warned, "is to see the Church as more important than its message" (*NYT* 3/28/02); and another acknowledged the "chronic shortage of priests in the US and elsewhere" (*NYT* 4/20/02). Church officials responded to priestly pedophilia not only by pondering the frailties of faith and deferring to established moral authority, but by making sure that, whatever their aberrant sexual behavior, pedophiliac priests should not, under any circumstances, be prevented from "doing their job" (ibid.).

For ideational reasons and material exigencies, church authorities responded to the evidence of sexual abuse by demonstrating sympathy and concern for priests, not for their putative victims: they suggested counseling rather than punishment (Barth 2010, National Review Board 2004). "Is anyone getting help for Father Diaz? He is experiencing a very difficult situation. Should we be doing more for him?" (*NYT* 4/20/02). These were the worries that Brooklyn Bishop Daily expressed about Father Diaz in private letters that circulated years before the revelations about the father's serial pedophilia became public. Although the behavior was widely known inside the church, Bishop Daily rarely mentioned it, instead commending Father Diaz for being hard-working and for "ministering during the past 25 years in the best international traditions of the Roman Catholic Church" (ibid.). He also noted Father Diaz's priestly kindnesses, pointing to the attestations of parishioners and not only to those of religious authorities. In all these ways, the bishop judged Father Diaz to be an "exemplary" priest (ibid.), no matter what later came to be publicly construed as his sexual crimes.

Intrainstitutional loyalties at $T_1$ are supported by interinstitutional suspicions and hostilities. The millennial distrust of ecclesiastical authority for the civil was manifest, for example, in Pope John Paul II's 2002 support for a letter that praised a French bishop who was willing to face prison rather than hand a pedophile priest over to the civil courts (*NYT* 4/30/10). In a 2001 article in the *Pilot*, Boston's archdiocesan newspaper, Cardinal Law – soon to become a central figure for having failed to report and discipline repeat offenders – suggested that, when victims of abuse turned to civil authorities, they prevented church authorities from dealing with the issue properly (*Wall Street Journal* [*WSJ*] 1/18/02). Speaking about his decision not to bring priestly pedophilia before the police, one bishop explained: "It would have been a great scandal, and all the energies of the church would have been spent dealing with those [who] would take advantage" (*NYT* 4/20/02).

## Code Switch

"What was most extraordinary to those of us who had long monitored the problem," two veteran reporters wrote about church pedophilia in 2002, "was the aura of surprise and discovery with which it was being covered in the news media this time around" (Bruni and Burkett 2002 [1993]: xviii).

That priestly pedophilia is heinous was the uncontested presumption, the ground base upon which that strain eventually became societalized; but it was neither the primary referent of the symbolic explosion nor its sociological trigger. Pedophilia was rather the pretext for writing a social text about the nature of civil obligation and the extraordinary dangers of failing to fulfill it.

The *Boston Globe*'s Pulitzer Prize-winning exposés of 2002 – the paper published nearly 300 stories in the first four months (Bradlee 2002: x) – code-switched the church's "hidden," intrainstitutional sexual practice, thus exposing it to the harsh light of a new day. However, the big news, the eye-catching disclosure that made "the dam ... burst," the revelation that "struck a nerve" (ibid.), was not the details of priestly pedophilia, but the *Globe*'s reporting that Cardinal Bernard Law had known about the practice for decades. "Church Allowed Abuse by Priest for Years" (*Boston Globe* [*BG*] 1/6/02), the *Globe*'s front-page headline screamed indignantly, the subhead explaining: "Aware of [Father] Geoghan record, archdiocese still shuttled him from parish to parish." The priest in question was John J. Geoghan, whom the *Globe* reported as having abused more than 130 young people "during a three-decade spree through a half-dozen Great Boston Parishes." But, even as Father Geoghan faced the first of two criminal trials for his actions, the *Globe* insisted that "details about his sexual compulsion are likely to be overshadowed by a question that many Catholics find even more troubling: Why did it take a succession of three cardinals and many bishops 34 years to place children out of Geoghan's reach?" (*BG* 1/6/02). Later that year, in the *Globe*'s book-length account *Betrayal: The Crisis in the Catholic Church*, Deputy Managing Editor Ben Bradlee Jr. framed the newspaper's journalistic accomplishment in much the same way: "A story about a priest who was accused of molesting children was now a story about a bishop who protected that priest [so that] the Church got to keep the ugly truth under wraps" (Bradlee 2002: ix–x). The *Globe*'s months-long reporting was represented simply as factual; and, certainly, it was based on painstaking research and guided by professional norms of journalistic objectivity. But moral judgments, not only empirical facts, were also in play – precisely because journalism is a key communicative institution of the civil sphere. Inside every one of the *Globe*'s factual descriptions, an interpretive framework was implicitly embedded.

Drawing on core civil values, media reports condemned the church's intrainstitutional values and actions as polluted, demonstrated the failure of its leaders to fulfill office obligations, and exposed the corruption of Boston's police and courts, decrying the dangers to sacred democracy that the once esteemed church now represented. The *Globe*'s investigative journalism detailed how the church responded to priestly pedophilia with strenuous efforts to keep knowledge about the practice wholly inside the walls of the religious sphere. Its critical reporting of institutional insulation evoked the vocabulary of anti-civil motives – secrecy, silence, manipulation, and deceit.

- "The Church's primary objective is clear – to avoid public scandal at whatever cost" (*BG* 1/31/02).
- "The Archdiocese for years dealt in secret with allegations" (*BG* 12/4/02).
- By engaging in "private negotiations" rather than public proceedings with the victims of pedophilia, the parties were "never brought ... near a courthouse" (*BG* 1/31/02).
- "Out of control clerical conduct [was] locked for years in secret Church files" (*BG* 12/4/02).
- "[Bishop] Daily asked them to keep the abuse secret" (*BG* 3/14/02).
- Family members were asked "to keep abuse secret" (ibid.).
- "Under an extraordinary cloak of secrecy, the Archdiocese ... has quietly settled molestations claims ..." (*BG* 1/31/02).
- "There is palpable unease ... about the cumulative effect of so many secret agreements" (ibid.).
- "The few who complained were invariably urged to keep silent" (*BG* 1/6/02).
- "Geoghan's free rein was made possible because the archdiocese said nothing" (ibid.).
- "The archdiocese has ... its secret archives" (*BG* 12/1/02).
- The "knowledge of sexual abuse ... will remain hidden" (*BG* 1/31/02).
- Religious leads "left a trail of international deceit and manipulation" (*NYT* 4/20/02)

Motivated by such anti-civil qualities, according to *Globe* reporters, church leaders succeeded not only in keeping sexual abuse hidden from the civil sphere but in keeping the evidence of their own "*oversight* failures" sealed inside court-sanctioned confidentiality agreements (1/31/02, italics added). In story after story, *Globe* reporters documented how church authorities had acted, not on behalf of powerless others, but on their own behalf. These failures were depicted as an abrogation of office responsibility that had undermined the possibility for civil control. "Someone in a supervisory role knew or should have known," the *Globe* (ibid.) observed, "but they did nothing to stop." *USA Today* (4/22/02a) affirmed that those in power "car[ed] more for their own image than [for] ministering to hundreds of victims" and the *New York Times* (3/28/02) noted that, by "covering up scandal [and] threatening those who wanted to speak out," church authorities misled the public.

Because institutional power was not regulated by civil office, the *Globe* (1/17/02) reported, the clergy "were exempt from the law." Ecclesiastical authority "had little to fear from the courts" (ibid.; see also *BG* 1/17/02) – "Cardinal Above the Law" according to Jay Leno's later ridicule. Because the civil sphere had left church authorities alone, the *Globe* (5/12/02) argued that judges were themselves "complicit in secrecy." An appellate court in New York, it reported, had once declared a pedophilia investigation "an impermissible inquiry into church doctrine protected by the freedom of religion" (ibid.). Refusing to give police investigators a warrant, another judge objected that it was "outrageous to search the home of a priest" (ibid.). With the office corrupted and the law in retreat, according to the *Globe*, "[c]hurch records were sealed behind a constitutional fire wall" (*BG* 11/23/02).

Two months after the *Globe*'s initial revelations, the *New York Times* (3/28/02) described "the reactions of Roman Catholic Church leaders" as "shocking." Public opinion, the sea within which civil institutions swim, had now become deeply offended. For many, perhaps even for the majority of Americans, Christian religion provides metaphysical anchoring for American democracy; there were now fears that America's center would no longer hold. Three months after the first stories were filed, the *Wall Street Journal* (6/13/02) reported that 68 percent of Americans believed the Catholic Church was covering up the sex scandal "instead of getting the facts out," and 89 percent were convinced that "Catholic bishops should be removed [from office] for transferring priests instead of calling the police." In its investigative retrospective, the *Globe* evoked neither sexual practice nor religion, stressing instead the foundational language of democracy:

> Boston may be the quintessential American Catholic city, yet the scandal soon proved to be far more than a local story. It

became an international story about how the rights of powerless individuals are pushed aside in the interests of a powerful institution, about how mortals can damage an immortal faith. (Investigative Staff of the *Boston Globe* 2002: 8)

Making an analogy with the United States' most egregiously anti-civil scandal of the twentieth century, the *Wall Street Journal* (4/18/02) asserted that the pedophilia scandal would "go down with Watergate ... as a textbook case of duplicity."

## Material Regulation

The civil sphere's communicative media had exposed the dereliction of office control inside the church. Office holders had failed to live up to civil standards, journalists reported; they had a "built-in conflict of interest" (*USA Today* 4/22/02a), as their intrainstitutional concerns opposed those of the social whole. The antidote was clear: religious leaders should report accusations of abuse to outside civil authorities, rather than leaving them to be dealt with inside the church (*WSJ* 3/18/02). If the church hierarchy was unfit for office, coercive civil authorities would have to take their place.

Regulatory authorities were quick to take up this call. The movement from the interpretative intervention of communicative institutions to the material force of regulatory intervention was sometimes extraordinarily direct. For decades, courts had allowed evidence of sexual abuse to be sealed behind confidentiality agreements. Now, in the wake of code switch and "acting on a motion by the *Globe*" (*BG* 1/6/02), courts ordered that files be opened to public scrutiny. Truckloads of documents were transferred physically from the Boston Archdiocese to the court's jurisdiction.

More typically, the movement from code shift to material sanction was less direct. To become visible, it had to be reconstructed by the media in heroic, dramatic terms.

[Massachusetts] Attorney General Thomas F. Reilly grew up in what he calls "a typical Irish Catholic family" ...

"We knelt down and said the rosary, as a family, every night," the attorney general remembered ...

> As a young prosecutor, Reilly learned of a priest who had sexually abused a child in Arlington, but he considered it an aberration. When the extent of the abuse committed by a former priest ... became known in 1992, Reilly said he was shocked, but he gave the church the benefit of the doubt ...
>
> Then in January [2003], as he read disclosure after disclosure [in the *Globe*] Reilly became furious ...
>
> "Where's the moral outrage?" ...
>
> Reilly fired legal shots at the church, *forcing* [Cardinal Law] and the archdiocese repeatedly to alter course.
>
> A week after [Cardinal] Law insisted there were no sexually abuse priests working in the archdiocese ... Reilly went public, saying that prosecutors, elected and accountable to the public, should be deciding the culpability of sexually abuse priests – not the cardinal. (*BG* 5/12/02, italics added)

The moral of this story was clear: only by displacing the authority of religious leaders could democracy be saved.

Shifting the location of the regulatory boundary that separates civil and religious spheres was the most far-reaching civil repair to emerge from the societalization process. Reporting a "legal watershed," the *Globe* (ibid.) declared that "[Bernard] Law became the first cardinal in the United States to be deposed over his actions as a prince of the church." In a victory for democracy over aristocracy, the civil sphere increased its sway, "holding the cardinal and other church leaders to a higher standard" (ibid.). Sex abuse was caused by office abuse, by the weakness of a key institution of the civil sphere. Church authorities were now placed more firmly under civil control. Grand juries of citizens were impaneled in large US cities – juries to which local district attorneys, legal representatives of the wider civil sphere, presented damning evidence not just of sexual abuse, but of profound institutional irresponsibility.

A 2005 report from Philadelphia's grand jury described dozens of victims and offending priests, asserting that the city's cardinal, the highest-ranking local church official, had "excused and enabled abuse" (*NYT* 6/14/12). The impaneled Philadelphia citizens issued 60 indictments against the city's churchly authorities. Abuse victims filed thousands of suits in US courts, more than 550 in California in one year alone (ibid.). With civil authority displacing religious authority, church funds came under judicial control. Five years after societalization, California's church had been compelled to hand over more than $200 million to plaintiffs, and four dioceses in mid-size US cities had filed for bankruptcy. A decade after societalization, legal fees alone were estimated to have cost the Catholic Church $2.5 billion. In the late 1960s, states had begun requiring caregivers to report suspected sexual abuse to police. Only now, a half century later, were such mandatory reporting laws extended to the church (Isely 1997: 292, Lothstein 1993, Myers 2008: 454).

These civil interventions into the religious sphere triggered "outrage in the pews" (*WSJ* 4/26/02) and among reform-minded religious authorities. The pressure opened up possibilities to institutionalize civilly oriented reforms from within, making office obligations more binding on power structures inside the church. As an angry Catholic laity stressed the internal, intrareligious nature of its indignation (*USA Today* 4/24/02), its members gave voice to a sense of quasi-civil exclusion from secret church hierarchy and formed civil associations to challenge it. As the editor of the conservative *Catholic World Report* put it, "[i]f American clerical leadership has been paralyzed, the ordinary faithful ... should take the lead" (Lawlor 2002). Victims' rights groups demanded greater accountability of church leaders to laity (*USA Today* 4/22/02b). Among these groups were the Committee for the Prevention of Clergy Sex Abuse and the Voices of the Faithful, the latter gaining some 19,000 members in its first six months in 2002.

In June 2003, the US Conference of Bishops approved the Dallas Charter. Local dioceses and religious orders were compelled to participate fully in the multimillion-dollar investigation by John Jay College of Justice, which led to a highly critical, widely distributed report on financial costs, abusers, and victims (*USA Today* 1/8/04). The charter also compelled every US diocese to set up review boards of laity designed to examine abuse claims, counseling officers for victims, a massive preventive education program (which eventually reached more than 6 million children), mandatory background checks on all adults working with children, yearly compliance audits, and a review board for auditing compliance at the national level (National Public Radio [NPR] 1/11/07; *USA*

*Today* 1/8/04, 11/18/04, 2/21/05). Pope Benedict was forced into an unprecedented early "retirement," under the shadow of the pedophilia scandal. His successor, Pope Francis, moved to defrock clerical pedophiles and to conduct quasi-civil trials inside the religious confines of the church-state (*NYT* 6/16/15), though Francis' own commitment to the civil reconstruction of religious authority was itself eventually questioned (*NYT* 1/18/18, 1/20/18a, 1/20/18b, 1/23/18).

## Backlash

As mounting civil pollution and sanction overwhelmed steady state, societalization made the intrainstitutional strategies of churchly authorities null and void. Yet, far from acknowledging the moral motivation of its critics, high church officers "often dismissed allegations of pedophilia by priests as an attack on the church by its enemies" (*NYT*, 7/2/10). Religious authorities made war against judgments from the civil sphere and institutional intrusions. After a critical meeting with Cardinal Law five months into the pedophilia scandal, the pope announced that the US cardinal was to retain his position. *USA Today* (4/22/02a) reported the pope's anxiety that intrainstitutional, churchly values were being abandoned in the face of civil pressure: there was "concern by the Vatican for appearing that the church is run by US public relation surveys, not its own standards of forgiveness, penance and restitution."

Denying the legitimacy of civil concerns, church authorities framed media code switching as strategic and self-interested. *La Repubblica*, the liberal Italian newspaper with extensive Vatican contacts, reported that "certain Catholic circles" suspected that "a New York Jewish lobby" was responsible for the media outcry, a veiled reference to the religion of the Sulzbergers, the family that owned the *Globe* and the *New York Times* (*NYT* 4/3/10). If not the media, then other entities were to blame for the critical publicity – anything and anybody other than the church itself. Decades earlier, Pope John Paul had worried out loud that publicizing sex abuse would only help "the Communists and the Protestants" (*NYT* 4/20/02).

During the more recent scandal, church officials blamed "social trends of the 60s" for having spawned "sexual license" and a relativist "corporate culture" of anything goes (*NYT* 3/28/02). The prominent Catholic theologian Richard John Neuhaus told *USA Today* (4/22/02a) that "pedophilia is not the issue; it's the general laxity in morals and doctrine that prevailed at the time when these (sex offender) priests were seminarians." The chief exorcist for the Holy See suggested that *New York Times*' coverage of Pope Benedict was "prompted by the Devil": "There is no doubt about it. Because he is a worthy successor to John Paul II, it is clear that the Devil wants to grab hold of him" (ibid.).

Just as powerful church elites refused to recognize their motives and actions as immoral in civil terms, they fought strenuously against external efforts at civil regulation. They claimed, for example, that victims' lawyers were pursuing lawsuits not for moral reasons, but merely for material compensation. As far as their own material interests were concerned, they quietly waged a full-court, state-by-state campaign against relaxing statutes of limitation, whose elimination would have greatly facilitated the civil prosecution of sex abusers (*NYT* 3/28/02).

Recalling the church's successful campaign to prevent Colorado from extending its limitations statute, one lawyer described "the politics [as] the most brutal thing I've ever been through" (ibid.). The campaign continued for years. A decade after the code switch, under the headline "Church Battles Efforts to Ease Sex Abuse Suits," the *Times* (6/14/12) reported one high church official's warning that nullifying statutes of limitation "would not protect a single child but would generate an enormous transfer of money to lawsuits to lawyers."

The extraordinary energy and resources the church devoted to resisting civil intrusion had significant effect. To sustain punitive regulation, the legal and police powers of the civil sphere must breathe the oxygen of public support. Because US legal sanctions are mostly organized locally, church officials worked to drum up "substantial parish and community support" for shamed and even convicted priests, and the punishments meted out were diluted accordingly (*NYT* 4/20/02). It was widely reported that, even as "civil authorities are pressing bishops to be more forthcoming," priestly abusers were being "treated delicately by law enforcement" officials, despite the church's refusal to speak about abuse in public or open up personnel files (ibid.).

Legal confrontations with the church were massively publicized, but criminal cases were consistently plea-bargained, not publicly tried. One Bronx prosecutor, commenting on what he viewed as an alarmingly gentle court decision, complained: "this only happened because this guy was a priest" (*NYT* 4/20/02). Of the 90 preventive measures the Kansas City diocese agreed to in 2008, only a minority were enforced (*NYT* 8/15/11). Even some provisions in the powerfully reformist Dallas Charter, passed by the National Council of Catholic Bishops in June 2002, were watered down by the Vatican before it went into effect at end of that year.

## Return to Steady State

On the fifth anniversary of the *Boston Globe* revelations that had triggered code switching, National Public Radio revisited the event, devoting to it consecutive reports titled "Scandal in the Church: Five Years On." The program's host testified to an historic movement from intrainstitutional darkness to civil visibility. "The *Boston Globe* revealed widespread abuse of children by priests and proof of a cover-up by the church," she recounted, referencing media intervention and the anti-civil character of office authority (NPR 1/11/07).

A contributing reporter attested that the Survivors Network of Those Abused by Priests [SNAP] still gets "calls from new victims every week" (ibid.), but emphasizes that such continuing abuse is now handled intrainstitutionally. An abuse victim who had become a member of the lay committee on clergy abuse for the Cincinnati archdiocese declared: "this is our church" and "our responsibility to yell and to scream" (ibid.). A decade later, the *Times* reported that "the United States Conference of Catholic Bishops said that from July 1, 2015, to June 30, 2016, it received 730 credible abuse allegations against 361 priests," and a lawyer representing current victims observed: "It's endless" (*NYT* 7/26/17). The strains remain, and so do the claims, but it is now the US Conference of Catholic Bishops that receives them.[1]

# 5
# Financial Crisis

## Steady State

That steady state is a social construction of institutional stability via boundary reciprocity rather than an objective measure of some actual conditions is exquisitely illustrated by the decades of equanimity about financial markets before the fall of Lehman Brothers on September 14, 2008.

For centuries, capitalist economies had been subject to cyclical recessions and periodic depressions, triggering reactions from the creation of national banks to controlling money and credit or to developing socialist policies that replaced capitalist markets altogether. Since the regulations of the 1930s, however, neither boom nor bust had prompted widespread anxiety about the self-correcting capacities of capitalism, much less a full-court reconsideration of the boundaries between civil sphere and market. The recuperation of postwar Europe and Japan, the dramatic increases in economic productivity with computerization, the end of state communism in the East and the privatization of state enterprises in the West, the globalization of capitalist production – all of these developments seemed to affirm, for observers not only on the right but on the center and even on the left, that serious economic destabilization was long since past. The effect of the increasing confidence that resulted was that, after decades of market intrusions that had pushed the boundary between civil and economic spheres to the left, the needle pushed to the right from the 1980s onward, allowing less regulated economies to be freer from civil control. State enterprises became private, competition was encouraged, and Keynesianism and monetarism became tools of what came to be called the neoliberal state. Socialism died, social democracy became New Labor, and only "varieties of capitalism" remained.[1]

Democratic states stripped regulations off their economies like old paint peeling on a hot summer day. It was during the Democratic administration of President Bill Clinton that the American government repealed Glass–Steagall, the Depression-era law that had forbidden mixing securities trading and banking under the same corporate roof. The rationale for that New Deal legislation had been to protect everyday citizens from what was considered the market's dangerously anti-civil predations, assuring not only the security of bank deposits but, more broadly, trust in the social relations that bind economic life. Economic authorities themselves were presumed to possess neither the character nor the ethical sense to guarantee societal-wide economic security. Such morality would have to come from the outside, from civil sphere ideals administered by agencies of state.

Decades later, the market had come to seem more civilized and tamed. "Nothing really bad had happened since 1982," one economist explained to *USA Today*. Indeed, in the decade after the repeal of Glass–Steagall, financial speculation by deposit-holding banks was applauded (*USA Today* 9/19/08). So were new efforts to "financialize" mortgage markets, facilitated by a new investment instrument called derivatives. Derivatives encouraged lending to debtors at super-low, subprime rates, which allowed high levels of leveraging among creditors in turn (Mann 2013: 129–78).

The intraeconomic dangers triggered by deregulation were widely discussed in the years before Lehman's collapse. These concerns, however, were largely confined to the economic pages of national newspapers and to specialized economic media (Starkman 2011, 2014), causing hardly a ripple in the broader public outside. Wall Street was largely depicted as "a trusted place to invest," as "the triple-A rated center of the financial world" (*USA Today* 10/1/08). While the US economy actually fell into recession in December 2007 (*NYT* 12/2/08b), neither candidate Barack Obama's warnings about economic instability nor his criticisms of deregulation policies gained traction. Until the final weeks of the 2008 campaign, the steady state was sustained.

## Code Switch

Lehman Brothers, the giant Wall Street investment firm, declared bankruptcy on Sunday evening, September 13, 2008. A government coterie of elite economic advisors had decided to cut Lehman loose, primarily for economic reasons (Williams 2010). After years of bailouts, too much was finally too much, and this time reckless loans would not be redeemed. If moral risk were not imposed, if economic punishment did not follow bad economic judgment, then capitalism as an economic structure could no longer be maintained. When Monday media reported on Lehman's crash, however, everything changed. Occurrence was transformed into event, and intrainstitutional regulation became hard to sustain. The code had been switched: the societalization of the financial crisis began months before the material consequences of the Great Recession were felt.[2]

Deregulation and the strains it produced (Mann 2013: 322–60) now came to be constructed not as economically productive, if risky, but much more broadly and negatively, as serious endangerments to the civil sphere. It was not just a matter of economic rationality or lack of it, but one of moral hubris and emotional humiliation; and a moral drama began to be played out. Under screaming, multicolumn, bold headlines on its front page, the *New York Times* (9/15/08b) described the precipitating event as having brought "once proud financial institutions ... to their knees." Moral judgment, not technical management, was at stake: the *Times* (9/19/08) ominously warned about the imminence of "judgment day," and President Barack Obama declared that the "day of reckoning has arrived" (*WSJ* 2/25/09; see also *USA Today* 2/25/09).

The media reported generalized anxiety about the future of society itself, not only a Wall Street crisis but one that was "filtering into the everyday lives of Americans, spawning confusion and anxiety, stoicism and black humor" (*WSJ* 9/19/08). *The Times* reported "fear" of "a precipitous decline," portending the "end of an era" (9/15/08b). Foundations would have to be rethought, boundaries between spheres – "the relationship between the government and the economy" (*WSJ* 9/24/08) – radically changed. Washington "had the feel of wartime" (*NYT* 9/19/08); the enemy was market instability, the "exotic securities" and "risky mortgages" that had resulted in "economic mayhem" (*USA Today* 10/1/08).

Economic elites, it now appeared, had failed to control this danger internally. In the context of apocalyptic anxiety and moral judgment, the US state began to inject massive monetary support to stabilize key financial institutions. Market managers themselves, along with their ideological and political supporters, believed such boundary breaching would be merely temporary. President George W. Bush articulated such a belief in a straightforwardly economic way: "The American people can be sure we will continue to act to strengthen and stabilize our financial markets and improve investor confidence" (*NYT* 9/18/08). Once the massive financial bailouts allowed economic managers to rewind the motor, problems related to the crisis would be handled internally and the steady state quickly restored. "The government has no intention of running" anything, a former chief economist of the IMF assured Congress. "This isn't France. This is temporary" (*USA Today* 9/19/08). The alternative scenario was unthinkable: that the political representatives of the civil sphere would not only lift the hood and change the oil, but mess around with the economic machine.

The case for a quick return to intrasphere control rested on the assumption that nothing important in the economic machine was fundamentally anti-civil. Richard Fuld, Lehman Brothers chief executive, assured a Congressional tribunal that his actions had been "prudent and appropriate" – despite the economic disaster they were later to create (*NYT* 10/6/08). Alan Greenspan, former Federal Reserve chair, acknowledged "misjudgments" but denied out of hand the possibility of "malfeasance" (*NYT* 10/23/08). The crisis happened because of a "flaw in our model," the fallen hero of America's era of deregulation explained (ibid.).

The flaw had created an anomalous "misalignment of interests" between investors and clients, such that the former could profit from risky loans while the latter suffered (ibid.). Structural adjustments might be necessary, Greenspan allowed, but interests would quickly be realigned and the machine easily fixed. When Democrats asked the Bush Treasury for bailout funds to help the 4.5 million homeowners scheduled to lose their homes, Secretary of the Treasury Hank Paulson refused to acknowledge such an obligation to the civil sphere. State funding was intended, the former Goldman Sachs president insisted, not to help the masses, but to fix the market for money: "We are actively engaged in developing additional programs to strengthen our financial system so that lending flows to our economy" (*NYT* 12/2/08a).

But code shift created outrage. The exploding sense that basic civil values were endangered blocked any easy return to the intrainstitutional handling of economic strain. Under the withering glare of the civil semiotic, financial practices were now seen as dark, dangerous, and deeply polluting, and public interpretation moved in a decidedly more antagonistic direction. It was not simply that "mistakes were made," the *New York Times Magazine* (1/22/09) fulminated. What had transpired was "grand financial malfeasance," an "industry-wrecking incompetence" whose "culpability" was "diffuse [and] colossal" and on an "awesome scale." *Rolling Stone* (7/9/09) depicted the financial industry as "a vampire squid wrapped around the face of humanity."

Leading economic actors were sharply attacked in non-economic ways. They had failed to protect humanity; they were not committed to a civil, solidaristic code. Two of their putatively anti-civil qualities seemed particularly galling. One was hedonism. Market makers were convicted of materialism and greed, of "torpedo[ing] the economy" through their "lust for excessive profits" and their inability to exercise self-control (*USA Today* 9/15/09). National papers ran articles demanding that the wealthy surrender their plastic surgery, caviar, and yachts (*WSJ* 9/20/08).

In a "massive moral failure," the "most powerful moneyed interests" were said to have "rigged the global financial system so that money managers, banks and a rarified class of institutional investors profited from massive high-risk schemes that beggared financial logic" (*USA Today* 9/24/08). The unregulated economy was analogized with "a vast gambling casino where the reward can be spectacular but always unpredictable" (*NYT* 12/16/08). Wall Street was described as having "Las Vegas ways" (*USA Today* 9/15/09). It was all about "rush and excitement," a "thrill of uncertain reward" that worked like "sex and drugs" on the human mind (*NYT* 12/16/08).

The other character flaw impugned by the public was arrogance. Those at the top of the economy had become bloated and complacent, believing themselves "too big to fail" (Sorkin 2009). Such hubris had been their undoing (Paeth 2012: 398, 494). One contrite financial wizard publicly confessed: "I used to be a master-of-the-universe kind of guy, but this cut me down to size" (*NYT* 12/16/08). The anti-civil qualities of hubris and greed were interconnected. Reporting on the conviction of Rajat Gupta, former head of McKinsey and Goldman Sachs board member, the *Times* interviewed a juror who worked as a youth advocate in Manhattan. She explained that Gupta's problem was "a need for greed" (*NYT* 6/15/12).

Economic managers received tongue lashings in thousands of articles, blogs, and television reports, their hedonism and hubris put blatantly on display. Public anger mushroomed over outsized bonuses that Wall Street investment firms still seemed intent on distributing. In the weeks between the 2008 election and his presidential inauguration, Obama felt compelled to label such bonuses "shameful," demanding that executives exercise "restraint" and declaring that "people on Wall Street still don't get it" (*USA Today* 12/14/09). Almost everybody else, it seemed, agreed (*USA Today* 6/11/09; *Financial Times* 1/30/09): the high and mighty who had wielded Wall Street power were now deemed unfit for office.

This code shift set the stage for repressive intervention on behalf of the civil sphere. If indeed bankers lived in a parallel universe, their world would have to be forcibly reconstructed: The "'fairy tale' of banking was over" (*WSJ* 10/10/08). No more separate worlds for business and democracy. There could be only one social universe; social justice and financial industry must somehow be combined.

## Material Regulation

In early 2008, President Obama signed a nearly trillion-dollar public investment bill designed, in some significant part, to keep markets lubricated and to shore up banks. Civil intervention, it was not yet civil reform. Soon enough, however, Congress initiated widely publicized hearings. Less informational than performative, they functioned as rituals of civil degradation. Vastly wealthy and formerly fantastically successful Wall Street executives were called on the carpet before political representatives of the outraged civil sphere and, amid groveling displays of public submission, promised to change their ways. Admitting their role in the undoing of the economy, many conceded the need for increased public oversight (*WSJ* 10/24/08).

Congress harshly questioned officials such as Alan Greenspan, who had been extravagantly praised during the economic boom. As chair of the Federal Reserve in the years before the bust, Greenspan had been charged with mediating the regulatory boundary between economy and civil sphere. He acknowledged now that he had allowed the latter to be dominated by the former. "The US regulatory system has got to change," Greenspan asserted. "People tend to fear what they don't understand and what is hidden from them, and a vast portion of the market is totally hidden from public investors. We have to know what the derivatives markets are doing, who owns what positions, what the hedge funds are doing" (*USA Today* 10/1/08). Less secrecy, more transparency, the people's right to know: civil sphere values needed to more deeply imbed in the economy.

As with societalization vis-à-vis church pedophilia, the translation of such communicative outrage into more organizational forms of regulatory intervention took two different paths. In the first and more immediate, condemnatory communication was translated into physical intervention and material sanction. Grand juries were activated to prosecute high-profile "insider traders." Between 2009 and the summer of 2012, 66 Wall Street traders and corporate executives were charged with crimes by the US attorney's office in Manhattan (*NYT* 6/15/12), the US winning convictions in every case that went to trial (*NYT* 12/31/12).

This wave of criminal prosecution produced a palpable, visible sense of civil intrusion into the economic sphere, the *Times* reporting that "the government has penetrated some of Wall street's most vaunted hedge funds and reached into America's most prestigious corporate boardrooms" (*NYT* 6/15/12). The newspaper framed the prosecutions as restoring a balance between spheres by instilling civil values inside the marketplace: "The government wants to protect investors, sending the message that the stock market is a level playing field and not a rigged game favoring Wall Street professionals" (ibid.).

The second response to code switching was more organizational: civil repair as restructuring. Regulative institutions interstitial between the civil sphere and financial markets (see Lee 2018, Olave 2018) had been in place at least since the New Deal; during the decades of deregulation, however, they had allowed market criteria to influence their economic decision-making at the expense of more civil concerns. The focus of repair was on strengthening the civil dimensions of office; those with economic power were to be made more responsible, more accountable to the members of the civil sphere, and not only to the functional needs of their own firms. When President Obama introduced his reform package in June 2009, he declared that "the American people sent me to Washington to stand up for their interests," not for the interests of the economic elite. To serve these interests, office obligations would have to be realigned, for "an epidemic of irresponsibility took hold from Wall Street to Washington to Main Street" and the "consequences have been disastrous" (*NYT* 6/20/09). As the *Times* (ibid.) explained, "Obama administrative officials argue that banking regulations in the past have had an inherent conflict of interest between ensuring the soundness of institutions and protecting consumers." The new legislation would expose polluted, anti-civil decision-making to the cleansing light of public concern, giving Washington "the tools to police the shadow system of finance that has operated outside the government's purview." Muscular intervention was the key to making office function in a civilly regulative way, giving "the Federal Reserve great supervisory authority over large financial institutions ... and expanding the reach of the Federal Deposit Insurance Corporation to seize and break up troubled units" (ibid.). Reenergizing office at the macro-, regulative level would have the effect of shifting the balance from functional to civil office obligations at the firm level as well. In late 2010, the *New York Times* headlined an economic columnist's open letter to Security and Exchange Commissioner Mary Schapiro: "Dear SEC, Please Make Brokers Accountable to Customers." The column suggested that new regulatory rules "would require stock and insurance brokers to put their customers' interests before their own" (*NYT* 11/19/10).

In its years-long struggle over such redesign, the Congress realigned interinstitutional boundaries, creating more symmetry between economic and civil interests. Capital requirements for banks were increased substantially and "stress tests" were put in place that demanded banks to prove their resilience to outside regulators. Glass–Steagall was not reinstated, but the Dodd–Frank Wall Street Reform and Consumer Protection Act was passed into law. At more than 15,000 pages, these regulations reached deep inside the financial system, establishing detailed directives about hedge funds, overseas investments, lending practices, derivatives, credit swaps, and more. After months of controversy, Dodd–Frank also put into place the "Volker Rule," designed to curb banks' proprietary trading, and created a massive new state organization, the Consumer Financial Protection Agency, with a legal mandate to protect the lay public from falling victim to the deceits of unbridled market power. This was civil repair of the economy on a scale not seen since the Great Depression.

As we will see in the next section, financial elites fought the rule-writing process every step of the way, challenging the implementation of Dodd–Frank and Volker tooth and nail and claiming that such civil intervention would cause irreparable economic damage. At the same time, however, financial elites initiated fundamental shifts in the internal organization of their institutions, a process that revealed a concerted effort to internalize (see Chandler 1977) and institutionalize civil repair via the creation of more civilly oriented office. The most conspicuous and far-reaching shift involved the vast expansion of "compliance." Civil repair could not succeed in the long term if it were to rely entirely upon the coercive imposition of outside force; more civilly oriented codes and procedures would eventually have to come not only from without, but from within (see Bruyn 2000). Compliance was the other side of implementation. "Next year is about one word: implementation," Gary Gensler, the chair of a new regulatory body, the Commodity Futures Trading Commission, told the *New York Times* (12/11/12):

> After spending three years and hundreds of millions of dollars attacking a bevy of new rules, Wall Street is begrudgingly gearing up for a new, if more mundane, phase of federal oversight. Regulators are ... leaving lawyers and compliance officials to steer banks through the new era. The specialists are drawing up training manuals and interactive programs to guide trainers, prodding regulators to clarify the minutiae of new rules ... "The banks say, 'We don't like the rules, but just tell us what they are and we'll figure them out,'" said Brian Gardner, a Washington research executive at KBW. The figure-it-out stage, analysts say, will define Wall Street's regulatory agenda next year. Banks like Morgan Stanley have been bulking up on compliance officers [and] holding two conference calls a month with clients to lay out the scope of compliance requirements. Goldman Sachs, like others, is testing computer systems it built to track derivatives trading.

One year later, on the fifth-year anniversary of the Lehman Brothers collapse, the *Times* headlined, in its White-Collar Watch section, "Companies More Forthcoming on Compliance." "In response to greater public scrutiny," the paper reported, the major Wall Street firms were "committing a lot more money and resources to comply with a host of regulatory requirements"; indeed, "it has become almost an arms race among companies to highlight how well they comply with the law" (*NYT* 9/17/13). JPMorgan, the largest investment firm on Wall Street, announced it would spend $4 billion and commit 5,000 employees to its compliance division, strengthening the autonomy of these new officials to follow the enormous inflow of new law and regulation (ibid.). Such internalization of regulation, the *Times* explained, appeared surprising, for it did not contribute to profit-making in the short run; in the long run, however, it provided ballast vis-à-vis external civil threats.

> Spending money on compliance is not something that will generate future revenue or directly enhance a company's profitability in the short term. Instead, like getting a flu shot, the money put into following the law and training employees *how to act properly* can result in benefits when the company does not have to pay for a future investigation and any penalties the government may seek to impose for a violation. (Ibid., italics added)

If they refused to lay out money for a flu shot when healthy, companies might get sick and lose a lot more. It was in order to realize their intrainstitutional values and interests that financial institutions empowered and reconstructed the compliance officer. The self-repair of non-civil institutions need not be sincere and idealistic: it just has to comply with what the civil sphere proclaims to be right.

To make sure they could properly comply, financial firms dangled fantastic compensation packages in front of powerful government regulators, to lure over to the other side the people who had been their institutional enemies. Less than a week after Congress sent Dodd–Frank to President Obama for his signature, the *Time*'s "Dealbook" headlined "Ex-Financial Regulators Get Set to Lobby Agencies," reporting that "nearly 150 lobbyists registered since last year used to work in the executive branch at financial agencies" (*NYT* 7/27/10). From that day on, the business pages were filled with reports about government regulatory experts changing sides. Three years later, under the headline "Former Regulators Find a Home with a Powerful Firm" (*NYT* 4/9/13a), the *Times* reported that Promontory Financial Group "is filled with so many former bureaucrats and political insiders that it has become known as Wall Street's shadow regulator" – "nearly two-thirds of its roughly 170 senior executives worked at agencies that oversee the financial industry."

One message sent by these new compliance officers was that Wall Street firms needed to engage in less destabilizing forms of financial speculation. Under the headline "Wall

Street Faces Specter of Lost Trading Units" (*NYT* 8/5/10), business journalists reported:

> They are the elite among the elite at Goldman Sachs, highfliers who are the envy of Wall Street. But on Washington's orders, Goldman is now considering a step that once would have been unthinkable: disbanding the corps of market wizards at the heart of its lucrative trading operation. Under the new Dodd–Frank financial regulations, Goldman must break up its principal strategies group, the wildly successful trading unit that has helped power the bank's profits. [And] across Wall Street, other financial giants are also embarking on the delicate task of complying with the new rules governing their trading and investments. Morgan Stanley is considering ceding control of its $7 billion hedge fund firm [and] at Citigroup, executives have sold hedge fund and private equity businesses … JPMorgan Chase has already begun dismantling its stand-alone proprietary trading desk.

"I think we have a very good structure in place that will diminish the likelihood of another collapse caused by financial irresponsibility," Barney Frank told a *Times* interviewer on the first anniversary of the bill bearing his name (*NYT* 7/20/11). The journalist reported, "Mr. Frank says Wall Street has gradually adjusted to the new reality," namely that "most banks have spun off their proprietary trading desks, as required, and many are overhauling their derivatives business" (ibid.). In what the *New Yorker* (5/16/16) called Wall Street's "new normal," banking was no longer as central to the US economy. Before the crisis, financial companies had accounted for nearly 30 percent of US corporate profits; as of 2016, the figure had fallen to 17 percent. When Morgan Stanley posted impressive 2014 first-quarter earnings, a leading market analyst remarked that the company had "got the memo early to reposition [its] business model for the post-crisis era" (*NYT* 4/17/14).

## Backlash

Here too, boundary shifting triggered blowback. What seemed like laudable civil repairs to energized and idealistic reformers appeared as sinister efforts at destructive intrusion to the economy's intrainstitutional elites. In the face of efforts at civil intervention, economic owners and managers pushed back hard, displaying righteous indignation. In what the *Times* headlined "A Show of Power," Jamie Dimon, president of JPMorgan Chase, lashed out against "the blanketing blame" of "indiscriminate vilification" (*NYT* 7/14/10). For financial elites, what they were facing was less reform than "revolution" (YouTube 2/19/09), not a matter of repairing but one of "blowing up the system" (*NYT* 6/17/09).

Against intense media pollution, massive reform regulation, legal assault, police action, and imprisonment, members of the economic elite strenuously defended their personal and professional integrity, demanding a speedy return to self-regulation. They warned that government oversight and control, while ostensibly protecting citizen interests, would actually create "moral risk," protecting economic actors from the consequences of bad market decisions.[3]

Many argued that it had actually been the remnants of earlier government regulation, not the newly unfettered economy, that had created the financial crisis in the first place (American Enterprise Institute 2011). At the end of 2009, a year that echoed with calls for broader social concern, the *Financial Times* (12/24/09) gave Goldman Sachs Director Lloyd Blankfein its Person of the Year award, praising him for holding steadfastly to market rationality and profits: "The Bank has stuck to its strengths, unashamedly taking advantage of the low interest rates and diminishing competition resulting from the crisis to make big trading profits."

When the Obama administration announced a housing bailout plan just one month after the president's inauguration, it was a gesture to social solidarity aimed at helping homeowners refinance mortgages and avoid foreclosure. Rick Santelli, reporting from the floor of the Chicago Board of Trade for the business channel CNBC, responded with a televised rant that "was quickly linked to and embedded in Web sites everywhere," charting backlash baselines that were later to inspire the Tea Party (*NYT* 2/20/09). Livid with outrage, Santelli warned that allowing civil values to imbed more deeply in economic life would undermine the market. It was a time for choosing sides, not for interlinking. To suggest that economic self-interest should be regulated, in the name of a wider social solidarity, would be a horrendous mistake.

> This is America! How many of you people want to pay for your neighbors' mortgage that has an extra bathroom and can't pay their bills! The government is promoting bad behavior [by] subsidizing the losers' mortgages, [for] people who carry the water rather than those drinking the water. (YouTube 2/19/09)

Far from being democratic, economic elites argued, financial reform was anti-individual and anti-liberal, lodging far too much power in the coercive state. The president of the American Bankers Association, protesting against the plan for a consumer protection agency, exclaimed that "banks are really dumbfounded by the scope of this [new] agency," suggesting "it's not like the current regulators don't [already] have all the authority they need" (*NYT* 6/17/09). Backlash leaders asserted that strengthening financial regulation had nothing to do with deepening the democratic obligations of office and everything to do with increasing bureaucracy, with constructing political power; it was not about regulating markets in the name of the people, but rather a "power grab" by the state (Competitive Enterprise Institute [CEI] 6/21/2012). "Dodd Frank aggregates the power of all three branches of government in one unelected, unsupervised, and unaccountable bureaucrat," argued C. Boyden Gray, former general counsel for the Bush administration, in a brief to the US District Court in Washington, DC on behalf of a lawsuit brought by the CEI (CEI 6/21/2012). Dodd Frank is a "tsunami," CEI's general council exclaimed – "all enveloping, hugely destructive, pretty much unaccountable" (ibid.). Far from representing the people, another CEI attorney explained, the director of the consumer protection agency "is like a czar. He is not accountable to anyone" (ibid.).

Under the headline "Obama Is from Mars, Wall Street Is from Venus," *New York Magazine* (5/22/10) recounted how financial elites had come to characterize the reformist US president: "redistributionist," "vilifier," "anti-wealth," "anti-capitalist," and "thug." After Dodd Frank became law and the Volker Rule proposed to prohibit banks from speculating with depositors funds, *The Times* (2/13/12) reported that, "with profits – and the future model of the industry – at stake," financial elites were launching their "broadest assault yet," accusing reformers of undermining not only market autonomy but capitalism itself. Two days later, an infuriated chief executive of a large bank drew a line in the sand: "Okay, first you slap us in the face, now you kick us in the balls. Enough is enough. I mean, we're done" (*New York Magazine* 5/22/10). The next year, in an article entitled "Trying to Pierce a Wall Street Fog," a *Times* economic correspondent reported on the war between civil values and market profits: "There was no question the banks did not want the CME [Chinese Mercantile Exchange] to make the market more liquid and transparent ... This was their cash cow and they didn't want to give it up" (*NYT* 7/20/13).

## Return to Steady State

During the years after Dodd–Frank became law, when regulators, staff, politicians, and lobbyists were down in the weeds of rule writing, right and left continued to fight their corner. Even as the right tried to block and repeal regulation (see the section "Backlash" in this chapter), the left fought to make it more intrusive (e.g. *NYT* 10/23/10, 5/1/11, 2/3/12, 4/9/13b). Each performed Clytemnestra, warning that, if their demands were ignored, the financial system was in imminent danger. They were mistaken. The financial system had been secured, for this demarcated moment of historical time. Societalization was over. There had been a return to steady state.

The goal posts had moved, but the game was still on. The boundary between economic and civil spheres had changed its location, but it was still a line, with the civil sphere on one side, market logic on the other. If regulations were the parameters, speculating, planning, risk-taking, and cunning were the variables that solved the equation of economic success. Strains continued to roil the financial sphere. "Danger signals" were sent in response to bad loans, heedless greed, secrecy, manipulation, and speculative bubbles (*NYT*

7/14/10). Relations between Wall Street and the civil sphere remained "skeptical," occasionally "confrontational" (*NYT* 3/20/15), but financial institutions were, once again, viewed more as "non-" than "anti-" civil.

Endless ideological wrangling paradoxically underscored the return to steady state. Partisan politics in capitalist democracies revolves, in some significant part, around where the boundary between civil sphere and economy should lie. Donald Trump's election to the nation's highest civil office, along with Republican control over Congress, gave conservatives the chance, not to overturn the new mediating institutions, but to hire their own personnel. At his confirmation hearings, the Republican nominee to supervise the nation's largest banks told senators he supported relaxing annual stress tests and exempting smaller banks from some regulation. Yet he also felt compelled to declare that "regulatory policies enacted since the financial crisis have improved the safety and soundness of the financial system," carefully adding, "as with any complex undertaking, after the first wave of reform, and with the benefit of experience and reflection, some refinements will undoubtedly be in order" (*NYT* 10/5/17).

# 6
# Phone Hacking

## Steady State

A steady state would seem more difficult to sustain when strains emerge not from institutions outside the civil sphere but from institutions within it. "Who will guard the guardians?" asked Lord Chief Justice Brian Leveson on the first day of the extraparliamentary inquiry into UK phone hacking that he directed (http://www.levesoninquiry.org.uk). Journalism is a key communicative institution of the civil sphere. It projects symbolic constructions of social reality, offering judgments of civil fitness in the guise of factual empirical descriptions (Alexander 1981, Alexander, Breese, and Luengo 2016, Schudson 1978, 2003). Such apparently empirical descriptions can support or undermine the legitimacy of intrainstitutional reactions to strain. How can moral outrage about a practice be triggered, then, if the very institution that communicates civil judgments practice is itself impugned? How will legal sanctions be imposed, if police – the material dispensers of civil punishment – are beholden to the very media elites that handle strains in an anti-civil way?

Possibilities for the internal corruption of journalism are ever present. News media depend on extra-journalistic resources to finance their reporting, and every subsidy to news production – whether from market sales, corporate and family ownership, or states – creates pressures that can compromise the medium's civil independence. Those who finance journalism, whether public or private, can in principle exercise anti-civil control. For their part, journalists organize self-regulating professional associations. Only if they gain autonomy from outside pressure can they interpret events critically, with reference to civil spheres, and in so doing achieve professional distinction (Alexander 1981, Alexander, Breese, and Luengo 2016, Breese 2011, Hallin and Mancini 2004, Schudson 1978, 2003).

For repair to become possible when anti-civil strains emerge from inside the civil sphere rather than from without, the civil sphere has to split, one part calling another to account for endangering sacred democratic ideals, one communicative medium exposing the corruption of another, one police unit calling out another's abuse of office, one organizational official condemning another as unfit to serve. In Britain, such a split has long existed among communicative institutions, pitting tabloid and broadsheet newspapers in heated and sometimes deadly fights. It is disagreement over how visibly fact and fiction are (or should be) intertwined that has so deeply divided Britain's tabloid and broadsheet newspapers. Certainly, the ideological inclinations of broadsheet media are evident: the *Guardian*, owned by a Scottish family trust, leans left; the *Times of London*, controlled by Murdoch's News International, looks right. Still, the news reporting of broadsheet newspaper aspires to professional journalistic norms, framed in a relatively complex and balanced manner (*Guardian* 11/2/11). Britain's extraordinarily influential tabloid media, by contrast, publish news accounts that are as much fictional re-creation as factual representation. Eschewing professional-cum-civil norms of transparency, sourcing, and balance, British tabloid journalism is replete with unattributed information, one-sided quoting, and exaggerated, sometimes fantastic revelations (*NYT* 3/16/89; *NYT* 7/21/11). Tabloid news is blatantly melodramatic, revolving around simplistic plots and clear narrative resolutions (*New Yorker* 4/2/12). Broadsheet newspapers report stories of public interest; tabloids devote themselves to human-interest stories (*Guardian* 11/2/11).

For decades, Australian-born magnate Rupert Murdoch owned two of Britain's most lucrative and powerful tabloids, the *News of the World* and the *Sun*, which together accounted for more than 5 million daily sales. Together with the *Times* broadsheet, which the family also owned, Murdoch controlled nearly 40 percent of Britain's daily newsprint market (*Guardian* 6/12/12). The conservative publisher reaped huge economic profit and potential civil power as a result.

In 2005, well-documented investigations publicly reported that Murdoch's tabloid newspapers were exercising their reportorial power in an anti-civil manner. The *Guardian* led a small handful of other British news media in revealing that Murdoch reporters had, as a regular and ongoing practice, hacked into celebrities' and royals' private cell phones, trolling for prurient information to splash over the front pages of the family's tabloids (*NYT* 9/5/10). Such civil intrusions into private life can be construed not only as undermining the institutional boundaries that sustain pluralism, but also as threatening the individual autonomy upon which contemporary democracies rely.

In the real civil society of 2005 Britain, however, these revelations did little to affect steady state. Instead, hacking was treated as an intrasphere matter. Egregious, paralegal methods of tabloid newsgathering had long been business as usual on Fleet Street. The black arts – spying, bribing, entrapping – had been an open secret for decades, with hacking widely perceived merely as a technological upgrade. The source of these phone-hacking allegations, moreover, was itself dismissed as lacking any civil standing: bitter hostility between broadsheet and tabloid was an old story (*NYT* 3/16/89). *Guardian* reports about Murdoch tabloid hacking were construed as routine manifestations of the endless political struggle between left and right. Finally, because the reported hacking victims were royalty and celebrities, they were portrayed not as civil victims but as arrogant members of Britain's elite.

The "steady as she goes" reaction to the 2005 hacking revelations was further sustained by the cooperation of Conservative parliamentarians and, more covertly, by Scotland Yard – the United Kingdom's Metropolitan Police.

After an abbreviated, largely pro forma investigation, just one *News of the World* reporter and one private investigator hired by that tabloid were tried and jailed for intercepting voice messages, and only a single parliamentary committee held hearings (*Guardian* 2/3/07, *WSJ* 7/20/11, 7/25/12). Tabloid owners and police directors alike reassured Britain's civil audience that there was no systemic problem, that it was only a matter of a few bad apples. Media self-control was maintained, for nothing broader and more systemic seemed at stake.

As a result of this maintenance of intrainstitutional control, phone hacking, as a widespread, putatively debilitating social practice, remained largely invisible to the broader British public. This appearance of steady state was sustained despite continuing efforts to push the practice into the broader democratic field. On July 9, 2009, the *Guardian* published another round of news stories questioning Murdoch journalists' civil ethics and for the first time raised flags about the professionalism of British police (*Guardian* 7/9/09). Yet, as before, these charges were persuasively challenged by aggressive ripostes from within influential corners of Britain's communicative and regulatory institutions.

On the afternoon of July 9, noting the media commentary, the Scotland Yard officer who had headed the earlier, severely abbreviated investigation, asserted: "I have no reason to consider that there was anything *inappropriate* in the prosecutions that were undertaken in this case" (statement by Keir Starmer in House of Commons 2010: Ev 455, italics added). Murdoch's *Times* opened its pages to the former director of Scotland Yard's Specialist Operations, who assured the British public that, contrary to *Guardian* allegations, the original investigation had "left no stone unturned" (House of Commons 2010: 8.108). Claiming that it had "seen no new evidence to suggest [widespread] phone tapping," the Press Complaints Commission (PCC), a semi-official national body charged with communicative mediation, lambasted the *Guardian* for speculation, declaring that "the PCC can only deal with the facts" (House of Commons 2010: 8.206). The implication was that the messenger was anti-civil, not the message. Such audacious efforts to depict *Guardian* reports not as news but as ideology were largely successful. Phone hacking was an institutional strain that continued to be handled in-house. While Scotland Yard had long known that the phones of thousands of ordinary British citizens, not just those of a handful of royals and celebrities, had been hacked (*NYT*, 9/5/10, Magazine), police leaders cooperated with conservative media elites to prevent this potentially deeply alarming fact from becoming public.

Such was the steady state maintained.

## Code Switch

The phone tapping of private citizens by tabloid reporters continued without disturbance until late 2010. An enormously profitable activity for tabloid owners, it was treated as routine practice not only by most of the media but by other UK elites (in police, politics, and business). With the steady state in place, phone hacking could continue to be handled in a manner that kept the practice intrainstitutional, hidden from public gaze. The boundary between phone hacking and the civil sphere seemed impregnable. The British media usually did not code-switch; when they tried, they found themselves unable to convince the British public to accept their critical interpretations.

What kick-started the stalled societalization of phone hacking was a series of journalistic judgments from outside the United Kingdom. In September 2010, more than a year after the *Guardian*'s second effort at excoriating civil judgment, reporters from the London bureau of the *New York Times* produced a voluminous, tightly sourced investigation that exposed not only the breadth of tabloid hacking, but significant corruption inside British regulatory institutions as well (*NYT* 9/5/10). The *Times*' revelations built upon the *Guardian*'s earlier reporting; its journalism significantly enlarged the scope and significance of the threat of hacking. *Times* reporters documented that, far from anomalous, hacking was a widely known practice among influential media elites and was covered up by UK police.

An ocean away from the ideological issues that divided UK newspapers and far removed from the political seductions and threats that had reinforced institutional boundaries, the powerful American newspaper proved a safer haven for British insiders to reveal hoary secrets about media hacking and police corruption. Compared with Britain's politically identified broadsheets, reports of these activities in the *New York Times* were also more likely to look like legitimate representations of social reality, to be taken as the kinds of free-floating objective facts that, in the very act of their description, effectively cast civil judgment. While the form of its reporting was factual, the *Times* characterized routine British media practices as shockingly anti-civil. The investigation described a "frantic, degrading atmosphere" among *News of the World* reporters, who "openly pursued hacking or other improper tactics" (ibid.). The *Times* suggested that Andrew Coulson, *News of the World*'s deputy editor, had created a "do whatever it takes mentality" that neutralized office obligations, fostering a selfish "hypercompetitive ethos" that prevailed over the civil ethos of more collegial and cooperative self-regulation (ibid.). Most explosively, the *Times* revealed that Scotland Yard authorities had withheld critical information from private lawyers and state prosecutors and that Scotland Yard's senior investigators had been compromised by "close relationships" with editors at *News of the World* (*NYT* 9/5/10).

Not just communicative institutions but, according to the *Times*, a wide range of the British civil sphere's regulative institutions had failed to perform in independent, critical, and democratically responsive ways. This was no longer only a story about "sleazy journalists," but also one about "crooked cops" (*USA Today* 7/22/11).

As in earlier efforts to maintain steady state, *News of the World* editors immediately sought to undermine the *Times* report. They suggested it had been motivated not by civil concerns but by "rivalry with a competing news company" (*NYT* 9/5/10); and they pointed to Murdoch's ownership of the *Times*' American rival, the *Wall Street Journal*. This time, however, such intrainstitutional efforts to undermine moral universalism failed. The *Times*' intervention into the British civil sphere did not, however, transform media phone hacking from an occurrence into an event; it did not set off an emotional and moral explosion. What the American paper's reporting did create, however, was a new set of "facts" that challenged intraelite contentions, a new interpretation that had the potential to undermine anti-civil controls.

Faced with the *Times*' more legitimate accusations of impropriety and moral degradation, Scotland Yard now felt compelled to reopen the investigation it had earlier declared closed. The same high police official who had summarily dismissed earlier *Guardian* reports acknowledged he had "decided that it would be sensible to look again at the matter, particularly since it appeared that the CPS [Crown Prosecution Service] might be required to give the MPS [Metropolitan Police] advice in relation to the allegations of the *New York Times*" (Leveson Report 2012: 9.13, Ward 2014). This meant that "new witnesses, who had been identified by the *New York Times* article, would have to be approached" (Leveson Report 2012: 9.13, Ward 2014). Scotland Yard mounted Operation Weeting and began contacting victims far and wide.[1] Private lawyers became emboldened, and began searching for clients who could plausibly launch legal complaints about being hacked. Any sustained police investigation depended, however, on the wider British public being mobilized and angry. This depended, in turn, on critical journalism inside the nation finally having its day.[2]

On July 4, 2011, two years after the *Guardian*'s second round of investigative reports and nine months after the *New York Times*' external intervention, a bombshell story transformed hacking from an intrasphere occurrence into an event that triggered a societal crisis. On the *Guardian*'s front page, below a color photo of a smiling red-haired teenage girl, a report declared, "the *News of the World* illegally targeted the missing school girl Milly Dowler and her family in March 2002, interfering with police inquiries into her disappearance" (*Guardian* 7/4/11; see also *Telegraph* 7/4/11). Milly Dowler's disappearance 10 years earlier had been widely represented – by broadsheet and tabloid, by left and right – as a deeply disturbing low point for British civil society, a heart-wrenching story of innocence destroyed by foul play. The wounding collective memory remained vivid, and Dowler's murderer had been convicted only 10 days before the *Guardian*'s July 2011 story.

What the newspaper now revealed was that Milly Dowler had not only been murdered but hacked.[3] The unfolding news narrative prominently featured such polluting accusations as "heinous" and "despicable." The Dowlers' lawyer characterized the hacking as "distress heaped upon tragedy," declaring that *News of the World* had "no humanity" (*Guardian* 7/4/11), adumbrating the boundary shift from institutional part to social whole. Milly's case was so offensive, it was reported, because she was an "ordinary citizen" rather than a rich celebrity already vulnerable to polluted construction (*WSJ* 7/13/11). "It's fair game to hack into politicians and celebs," London journalism professor Ivor Gaber told the *Wall Street Journal*, "but once you hack into a murdered teenager's phone it is different" (*WSJ* 7/14/11).

The revelation "turned a long-simmering problem into an explosive scandal" (*WSJ* 7/25/12). Britain's media described, and at the same time predicted, a "political firestorm" that would destroy everything in its path (*NYT* 7/21/11). The *Guardian*'s construction echoed like a thunderclap through communicative institutions in the British civil sphere, careening back and forth among blogs, radio, television, and print. Far from being routine, phone hacking was now connected to the heart of the anti-civil profane. The Dowler hacking was broadly characterized as a "revelation" rather than simply as new information (*Guardian* 7/4/11, 7/13/11, 12/15/11) – a desecrating evil long hidden by malevolent powers. In an opinion piece in the *Guardian* (7/8/11b), one outraged academic observer claimed that "the degree to which the *News of the World* profaned what many people take to be sacred is unprecedented in postwar media history." He continued: "The transgression of the *News of the World* and News International is not simply that they acted 'unethically' (in a narrow professional sense), or even illegally [but that] the actions of people associated with the *News of the World* became profanations, an evil polluting ... cherished sacred significance."

By the end of the "dramatic day of unfolding developments," what was now referred to as the "phone hacking crisis" was described as "*enveloping* the *News of the World*" (*Guardian* 7/5/11, italics added) – a declaration, whose factual status was not challenged, that intrainstitutional power had finally been superseded. In the words of Murdoch biographer Michael Wolff, the scandalous news demonstrated that "[h]acking is not at all an aberration, or a what-were-they-thinking error of judgment and strategy, but an expression of [News Corp.'s] fundamental identity: It's not just that they did it, but, more importantly, this is what they do" (*Adweek* 6/20/11). There was wide public support for a prominent Labor MP's framing of the intrusion as not only a "despicable" but an "evil act" (*Telegraph* 7/4/11).

In the days that followed, other "revelations" emerged. Murdoch's tabloid had also hacked into telephone calls among families of Britain's "7/7" terror victims and into conversations between families and British soldiers in Afghanistan who were later to die in combat (*Guardian* 7/5/11). Such accounts "further shocked the public," which "reacted with horror" to what a former soldier characterized as a "sordid investigation by journalists" conducted "to make monetary profit" (*Guardian* 7/6/11). The *Telegraph* (7/7/11) spoke of "the sanctity of the precious phone calls home," asserting that hacking "violated personal life." The *Times of London* broadsheet and *Daily Mirror* tabloid both headlined "Hacked to Death" (*Guardian* 7/8/2011a). The civil sacred and the economic profane were now being dramatically juxtaposed.

The hacking of innocents was traced to rich and powerful media barons. For almost a decade, the tabloid elite had managed to keep its hacking activities below the radar of the civil sphere, bribing police, issuing false statements, and representing its accusers as self-interested competitors, if not democracy's enemies. Once societalization transformed hacking into anti-civil evil, however, the Murdoch group felt compelled to camouflage itself in civil clothes. In 2009, a *News of the World* editor had comfortably lied to the parliament, assuring those elected representatives of the civil sphere that "no evidence of wrongdoing had been uncovered" by the paper's internal investigations (*NYT* 9/5/10).

In the midst of the subsequent societalization, such head-on resistance would almost certainly have undermined Murdoch's civil status and gravely injured his companies. The Murdoch camp decided instead that public deference to civil power must be paid. Murdoch editor Rebekah Brooks called the activities "appalling," claiming to be shocked by revelations about tabloid conduct she herself had directed (*Guardian* 7/5/11). Murdoch's media company, News International, stated it would be "absolutely appalled and horrified" if the charges were true, promised total cooperation with any and all inquiries, whether from Leveson, police, or parliament, and for good measure announced an internal investigation of its own (*Guardian* 7/6/11). When called to testify before parliament, Murdoch declared: "This is the most humble day of my career. To say I'm sorry is not enough." Describing his emotions upon hearing the allegations about Milly Dowler, Murdoch claimed, "at no time do I remember being as sickened as when I heard what the Dowler family had to endure – nor do I recall being as angry as when I was told that the *News of the World* could have compounded their distress" (*USA Today* 7/20/11).

The Murdoch elite's most audacious performance of civil degradation came on July 9, when News International shocked the British citizen audience by announcing that *News of the World* would be shuttered. After 168 years of publication, the tabloid had become transformed from a "British institution" symbolizing "brash populist British journalism" (*Guardian* 7/9/11) into a collective representation of extralegal surveillance at the very heart of anti-civil darkness. News International presented its decision as an act of purging and repentance, going so far as to order that the revenue from the tabloid's last issue would be donated to "good causes" (*USA Today* 7/8/11).

During face-to-face meetings with departing *News of the World* employees, ostensibly private but widely leaked, it was reported that Murdoch and his editors had actually told journalists they were "heroes," praising their "great work" in producing a "brilliantly professional newspaper" (ibid.).[4] Despite the civil sphere's onslaught against his journalistic practices, and despite his own public mea culpa, privately Murdoch was not repentant; holding his cards rather than folding them, he was waiting to push back. Indeed, closing *News of the World* was widely perceived as a strategic move aimed at staunching the flow of Murdoch's corporate blood, not as an authentic performance of civil amends – "more an act of survival than one of contrition" (*USA Today* 7/26/11). Rather than believing Murdoch's new-found profession of obligation to the civil sphere, observers publicly suggested that his real ambition was to maintain British government support for his company's proposed takeover of the British Sky Broadcasting (BSkyB), the most lucrative private television company in the United Kingdom (*Guardian* 7/13/11).

No matter how politically strategic and economically competent Murdoch the person, however, Murdoch the symbol had become submerged up to its figurative neck in anti-civil muck. An editorial in *The Daily Mail* headlined "Hubris and a Threat to Press Freedom" (*Guardian* 7/8/11a). The "ageing media mogul" had planned to "hand control [of BSkyB] to his youngest son," who would become the new head of the Murdoch "clan" (*Guardian* 7/8/11a). But they could now "see the writing on the wall," the *Guardian* claimed, and "these guys are on the run" (*Guardian* 7/13/11). Government spokespeople announced that Murdoch's bid for BSkyB was dead in the water. News International withdrew its takeover offer. Once lauded as a brilliant businessman and populist visionary, Murdoch was now portrayed as a greedy, anti-democratic, imperial tyrant. Under the headline "Murdoch Facing Parliament's Ire in Hacking Case," the *New York Times* (7/6/11) reported: "from all sides of the House of Commons, the disgust came thick and fast." A Labor MP declared: "We have let one man have far too great a sway over our national life"; and a Conservative colleague immediately agreed: Murdoch was guilty of "systemic abuse of almost unprecedented power" (ibid.).

The code had been switched, steady state was a thing of the past, societalization was the order of the day.

## Material Regulation

The aftershocks of the Milly Dowler explosion had finally forced a British code switch. The ensuing tsunami of public opinion compelled civil intervention, the *Guardian* (7/13/11) declaring – with scarcely concealed satisfaction – that the revelations of tabloid wrongdoing had "deeply affected public opinion and therefore galvanized parliament and even government." Phone hacking had finally been construed as a threat to democracy, as a practice motivated by profit, not by truth, and as one that threatened individual autonomy. Office regulation had failed. Murdoch's own broadsheet, the London *Times*, declared that the failure to morally construe the office reflected a dangerous chasm between media power and the values of the civil sphere: "The first rule of newspaper ethics, as with the ethics of political life, is not to lose touch with the moral codes of the audience: common sense, goodwill help to neighbors, decent conduct in general" (*Guardian* 7/8/11a).

If the public's power of interpretation were to be protected from anti-civil interference, UK media would now have to be regulated not only internally, by its own extrainstitutional elites, but externally, by rejuvenating the civil regulation of office. The material, coercive elements of the civil sphere intervened to punish and remove members of intrainstitutional elites, those who had earlier professed to be acting in the name of the civil sphere itself. Challenged by media revelations about its own corruption, Scotland Yard and regional police forces now moved to examine tens of thousands of pages of notes and millions of emails, demanded hundreds of interviews, and invaded business offices and private homes, searching for evidence of anti-civil conduct. They also made some 100 arrests, including of Rebekah Brooks and Andrew Coulson; of the chief reporter at another Murdoch tabloid, the *Sun*; and of a defense ministry official – all of whom were charged with "conspiracy to commit misconduct in public office."

Describing the rationale for a jury's decision to convict a Scotland Yard chief inspector, the *Guardian* (1/13/13) depicted her as "guilty of misconduct in public office" and quoted a high-ranking Scotland Yard authority declaring "it is a great disappointment that a detective chief inspector ... should have abused her position" and insisting that "there's no place for corrupt officers ... in the Metropolitan police service." A long string of other editors and reporters who had worked at *News of the World* and other tabloids, and a number of detectives and senior investigators at Scotland Yard, were arrested as well (*WSJ* 11/21/12).[5] Many eventually went to jail, including Coulson, who was sentenced to 18 months. Powerful editors, as well as local and national police authorities, were forced to resign. Hundreds of hacking victims brought lawsuits that eventually cost the Murdoch media company one billion dollars.

In the earliest days of the crisis, as the visible civil interventions exploded, political figures outside government and influential journalists and intellectuals demanded an official inquiry. When an already existing parliamentary select committee declared its intention to intensify its hearings, this was widely judged not to be enough. Only an independent, extraparliamentary commission, it was argued, could defend the interests of "society" against the particularistic interests of money, party, and ideology. On July 6, Prime Minister David Cameron acceded to this demand for the further exercise of civil power. Proposing that an independent inquiry be commissioned, Cameron instructed the Speaker of the House to make a vote on its creation a matter of free debate instead of party discipline, describing it as "an issue that united all three political parties" (*Guardian* 7/13/11).

Six days later, Cameron appointed Lord Justice Brian Leveson as chair of the inquiry, with power to summon witnesses and require them to testify in public and under oath (http://www.levesoninquiry.org.uk). Journalists described Leveson as an iconic embodiment of impartial judgment and civil duty – "not a great socializer" but "tough, persistent and industrious" (*Guardian* 7/24/11). Deputy Prime Minister Nick Clegg linked the Leveson appointment to civil purification, describing a "once-in-a-generation chance to clean up the murky underworld of the corrupted relationship between police, politics, and press" (*Guardian* 7/24/11).

Five months later, when Lord Leveson publicly opened the inquiry, he represented its task as a moral obligation imposed by the idealizing aspirations of the civil sphere, stressing the relationship between journalism, regulation, and social solidarity: "The press provides an essential check on all aspects of public life. That is why any failure within the media affects all of us. At the heart of this Inquiry, therefore, may be one simple question: who guards the guardians?" (http://www.levesoninquiry.org.uk). Six months later, while the Leveson Inquiry was still toiling away, this question was answered by the House of Commons Culture Media and Sports Committee, which reported its own phone hacking investigation as having exposed a dangerous failure of office:

> Rupert Murdoch … exhibited willful blindness to what was going on in his companies and publications. This culture … permeated from the top throughout the organization … speaks volumes about the lack of effective corporate governance at News Corporation and News International. We conclude, therefore, that Rupert Murdoch is not a fit person to exercise the stewardship of a major international company. (*NYT* 5/1/12)

In response to such massive civil intervention, both communicative and regulative, the "unspoken laws of tabloid news," unchanged for centuries, were now "reconfigured" from within (*NYT* 11/30/15). Rupert Murdoch testified to state authorities that he had "spent hundreds of millions of dollars in an effort to clean up," asserting "we are now a new company, and we have new rules, new compliance officers" (*Congressional Record* 1999). No doubt puffed up and self-serving, there is also no doubt that such organizational repair was real and that it effectively compelled editorial authority to be exercised in a manner more responsive to civil codes and less to the whims of readers and private profit.

Four years after code switch and civil intervention, the *New York Times*, which earlier had played a pivotal role in triggering societalization, offered an assessment of such claims. It found, indeed, that tabloid journalism had deeply changed. "The few drug and sex stings still orchestrated by [tabloid] newspapers," the newspaper reported, were now "subject to heavy legal scrutiny," being "justified by the papers [only] on the grounds that they have a public purpose beyond prurience" (*NYT* 11/29/15). Journalists were now instructed to "consult a member of the in-house legal team" before engaging in aggressive investigative tactics (ibid.). Tabloid reporters, who had once been "bullied by their editors into using dubious methods to get scoops" (ibid.), were now formally instructed about their civil obligations and rights.

> [Murdoch's] News UK[6] set out new rules for its reporters on topics like bribe [*sic*] public officials (do not), paying for stories (only sometimes), using private investigators (only with approval) and collecting private information electronically (do not do that, either). Employees are also required

> to have training on conflicts of interest, bribery, technology, workplace conduct, electronic communications and whistleblowing. (Ibid.)

"The tabloids are becoming less tabloidy," a leading UK media scholar observed (*NYT* 7/24/14). "The British press has had to clean up its act," acknowledged a former tabloid editor (Lyall). According to a former editor of the *Guardian,* who had guided the anti-Murdoch paper throughout its phone-hacking revelations, "[t]he days of the Wild West" were over (*NYT* 11/30/15). National Public Radio media correspondent David Folkenflick offered this verdict: "It really took this scandal to change the dynamic, there, of this incestuous nature of the newspaper barons and executives with the top law enforcement officials and the top politicians" (WBUR 2014).

## Backlash

By the time the Leveson Inquiry was in full swing, Murdoch and the tabloid elite were no longer performing contrition. "I take a particularly strong pride that we have never pushed our commercial interests in our newspapers," an unrepentant former managing editor of the *Sun*, a Murdoch tabloid, told reporters after being acquitted of bribing the police (*Guardian* 4/25/12): "It has now been exposed for what it is – a politically motivated witch hunt against tabloid journalism" (*Guardian* 4/27/15). Even as it faced massively intrusive efforts at civil exposure and punishment and initiated significant, deep-going reconstruction, the institutional elite began furiously pushing back. "A truly grotesque amount of taxpayers' money has been spent" on Scotland Yard's investigation into phone hacking, a now unrepentant Murdoch retorted to ferocious interrogation by Leveson counsel Robert Jay, who had put it to him that "your main objective [was] to improve the commercial appeal of these papers and you weren't really concerned with the ethical side" (*Guardian* 4/26/12a). Yes, *News of the World* had engaged in phone hacking, the mogul replied, but senior editors had ordered the practice; he himself had been "misinformed and shielded" (ibid.). Indeed,

Murdoch maintained he had upheld the highest standards of office: "I do try to set an example of ethical behavior and to make it quite clear that I expect it" (*Guardian* 4/25/12). Against the charge of deceit, he insisted that his intent as a media owner was "always to tell the truth, certainly to interest the public, to get their attention, but always tell the truth" (*Guardian* 4/26/12a). The *New York Times* (4/26/12) reported that the Leveson "questioning seemed almost deferential and genteel," in marked "contrast" to Murdoch's appearance "before Parliament last year."

Murdoch's turnabout presaged intense pushback from a newly united media elite. Deep civil anxieties about phone hacking had triggered the creation of the Leveson Inquiry, but what came out at the other end, 14 months later, seemed more like a proposal to strengthen the state, not the civil sphere. At the end of its four-volume, 2,000-page report, Leveson proposed, with great fanfare, a royally chartered commission with the power to prevent media abuse, first by issuing warnings against journalists and news media, then by issuing civil judgments and backbreaking fines.

The proposal's particulars shifted over the next two years, allowing the new regulatory power to be mediated – its opponents would say camouflaged – by three different layers of proposed organization (*Guardian* 10/10/13). But the message stayed the same: the media should be put on a governmental leash. Leveson's proposal would protect not simply against phone hacking, a practice now exposed and punished, but against whatever media activities this newly created governmental body deemed to have crossed the line.

The political and intellectual left, if a bit reluctantly, maintained that this would be all right; if the media were an industry like any other, then regulating it would serve the people's interest. Those inside the media, whatever their ideology, mostly disagreed. They indignantly declared that the media were not just an industry, but a civil institution. Editors, publishers, and reporters labeled the proposed regulation a "*politicians*' charter," shockingly tone-deaf to the needs, interests, and meanings of journalism (Ward 2014, italics added). "The newspapers have adopted an attitude of defiance," an LSE media watcher blogged (Media Policy Project Blog 1/8/14). Local newspaper groups went public with fears that the new system could "open the floodgates to compensation payments," place "a crippling burden on the UK's 1,100 local newspapers," and inhibit "freedom of speech and the freedom to publish" (*Guardian* 4/26/12a). National newspapers stridently warned against any further weakening of journalism in the brave new world of digital news.

Democracy now seemed threatened not by anti-civil tabloid media, but rather by the media's critics. The boundaries between civil sphere and state were back in place. What had once been conceived of as the final fruit of civil repair was now constructed as a threatening, intrusive, and anti-civil state. During his Leveson testimony, Murdoch had warned the inquiry "to be cautious when contemplating regulation," averring that "the press guarantees democracy, and we want democracy not autocracy" (*Guardian* 4/26/12b). The cunning media magnate was proven right. The tables had turned. Intrainstitutional self-regulation was now being defended in the name of democracy itself. Murdoch's exercise of his own power was secure.

## Return to Steady State

Leveson outlasted the scandal that triggered it and the civil repairs made in response. The inquiry had been commissioned in the immediate wake of code switching, during the molten heat of civil indignation. The commission publicly convened, however, only five months later, after hundreds of arrests had been made, dozens of public apologies proffered, and urgent fears for the center abated. While managing to uncover bits of new information, moments of riveting revelation were rare. A total of 337 witnesses were heard and counted, yet, although their testimony sometimes generated pity, it failed to generate the pathos of inflamed civil judgment. Far from becoming a media event whose compulsive viewing interrupts regular broadcasting and everyday routines (Dyan and Katz 1992), the Leveson hearings streamed on an obscure cable channel, Parliamentary TV, sustaining only a cult viewing as a result. The inquiry had become a spectacle for the curious, not civic ritual but mundane record.

Civil outrage had declined. The proposals that Leveson had tabled triggered furious pushback from journalists and publishers, who defended the intrainstitutional control against outside intrusion from a meddling, insensitive state. The boundaries between civil and non-civil spheres were back in place. The Conservative government shelved its promises to initiate civil repair (*Guardian* 4/21/16, 11/1/16, 12/22/16), and the reposts from its political opponents were lackluster (*Guardian* 4/13/15). Such was the return to steady state.

# 7
# #MeToo

## Steady State

#MeToo societalized sexual harassment in the workplace. Throughout the history of modernity, such sexual mistreatment had been almost entirely insulated from the civil sphere, safely hidden from its reach. This compromised the civil sphere, too, limiting its utopian qualities – freedom, equality, and solidarity – by defining them in a gendered manner that gave men sexual power over women.

For much of the civil sphere's history, women were not part of it. They participated almost exclusively in the domestic sphere of emotional intimacy, parenting, and reproduction, and inside this non-civil sphere they were subject to the authority of men – an institutional elite, a class, a status group, a patriarchy that defined the values, dominated the subordinates, and regulated their actions and interests. Not only work outside the home but sexual relations inside it were male prerogatives. If women suffered – and they often did, sometimes quite horribly – their cries were not heard by the wider society. Because they were marginalized, their suffering could not be societalized. Even when female subalterns were beloved – and they frequently were – they were deemed fundamentally non-civil: irrational, hysterical, weak, dependent, secretive, unable to stand up for themselves. Without a moral and legal civil standing, let alone an institutional one, women were not accorded a role in determining their sexual relations. They could not speak publicly – or even privately – about their sexual lives. Even when they made efforts to resist male sexual domination, their efforts were routinely dismissed as insincere, as strategic, perhaps even as seduction in disguise.

Feminism initiated the civil repair of patriarchy, breaking through the wall that had been erected between civil and intimate spheres and reconstructing the status of women (Alexander 2006: 235–64). First- and second-wave feminism were not only political movements concerned with mobilizing power, or legal efforts to expand citizenship; they were also, and perhaps above all, cultural efforts to redefine the nature of womanhood (Alexander 2001) among marginalized women, and also for male core groups themselves. If women were conceived of as rational, they would be allowed to vote; if autonomous, they could own property; if open and honest, they could enter into public life; if strong, they could work outside the home. Feminism challenged the civil representation of masculinity, creating counternarratives that polluted male domination. Claiming that men were less paternal than patriarchal, less concerned with loving and caring than exercising power and control, feminism created affecting, melodramatic stories about the pathos of sexism, about women as an oppressed class, and about courageous female heroes fighting against it.[1] Feminism sketched a new utopia of gender civility, of a world defined not by hierarchy and coercion, but by horizontal and consensual relations between women and men.[2] Feminist political and cultural performances transformed the consciousness not only of women but of many men as well. Those who scripted and acted out these performances became honored not only as successful strategists but as civil heroes – Elizabeth Cady Stanton, Betty Friedan, Gloria Steinem, to name only a few.

If second-wave feminism in the late twentieth century effected revolutionary transformations, however, its success was far from complete. Feminist social and cultural movements became routinized, and the societalizing episodes that marked effervescent moments of civil repair eventually returned to steady state. Feminism allowed women to move out of the domestic sphere and into the workplace, but many social problems associated with patriarchy remained. In the economic arena, women were still broadly subject to male power and frequently to sexual taunts, threats, coercion, and physical violation. Women were in the workforce, but they were still not fully fledged members of the civil sphere. In principle, they had access to legal rights and other protections of civil regulation; in practice, they remained second-class citizens, vulnerable to arbitrary practices that violated democratic principles. Female employees were often represented as intellectually inferior and emotionally immature, rationales that allowed male supervisors to slight them as workers and to focus on their sexuality. Women's accounts of their mistreatment were usually ignored; when their stories were attended to, they were rarely believed. Male domination had moved from the sphere of intimacy to the institutions of economic life, and it remained largely insulated from civil surveillance. Men occupied most of the higher positions, made the big bucks and the big decisions; women were underneath, supposedly fortunate to be there at all.

In the 1980s and 1990s, women appearing before the Georgia state legislature were subject to catcalls and whistles, a practice so routine that women created an idiom for it – "talking under your dress" (*Atlanta Journal Constitution* 3/16/18). A female state legislator who had served since the 1980s recounted: "it was almost an unspoken rule [that] it was no big deal, it was just for fun. It was always couched as a joke. At that time, sexual harassment was not really a word" (ibid.). Sexual harassment wasn't a "word" because male prerogative in the workplace – mental, moral, organizational, and sexual – was considered mundane and routine. "The fact that this is so prevalent," a Colorado woman complained, "so pedestrian that it no longer stands out when it happens, is inherently wrong" (*Colorado Springs Independent* 11/8/17a).

In the decades preceding #MeToo, everyday male behavior inside workplaces was episodically polluted as sexual harassment. A scattering of powerful men in politics (*WP* 12/7/17), entertainment (*Hollywood Reporter* 5/3/18), and science (Huffington Post 4/7/11) were exposed, morally sanctioned, and forced out of public life. They were represented as a few rotten apples, men who had stepped over the line; the very sanctioning of these men demonstrated that the bushel was mostly filled with good fruit. Sexually aggressive men who stepped up to the line but not over it continued to be described, with envy and barely muted admiration, as "womanizers." Women's stories of outrage and injury, let alone efforts at legal redress, continued to be routinely pushed aside. In New York City, in 2015, Ambra Battilana Gutierrez came to the police with an inflammatory accusation against Harvey Weinstein. She was wired for her next meeting with Weinstein, and returned with an incriminatory audiotape (*NYT* 10/17/17). Yet the office of Cyrus Vance, Jr., the Manhattan district attorney, declined to press charges. "We had the evidence," attested an official who had been involved in the investigation, "more than enough evidence to prosecute Weinstein"; and he talked about it "as a case that made me angrier than I thought possible, and I have been on the force a long time" (*New Yorker* 10/10/17).

Such was the insulation of the steady state. Only societalization could transform such routine behavior into something polluted and profane.

## Code Switch

The regulatory institutions of the American civil sphere remained quiescent, but the communicative institutions began to bridle with resentment and to stiffen with investigative ambition. In winter and spring 2016, as Donald Trump vanquished his rivals for the Republican presidential nomination, the incendiary far-right politician unleashed venomous attacks on mainstream news media, accusing them of creating false facts, threatening them with bankruptcy, even offering support to physical assaults on journalists. As the ideal and material interests of the communicative elite came under increasing threat, the media publicly interpreted some right-wing leaders not merely as anti-civil in the political–ideological sense, but as exercising sexual domination.

## Polarization Blocks Societalization

Candidate Trump dragged behind him a kite's tail of brazen womanizing, represented in mainstream journalism as part of his bullying, bragging, and abusive anti-civil persona. In early October 2016, the *Washington Post* revealed a decade-old tape recording of Trump boasting to a celebrity-news reporter: "When you're a star, they let you do it. You can do anything ... Grab 'em by the pussy. You can do anything" (NBC News 10/7/16). These misogynist boasts were immediately denounced, not only by leading Democrats but by mainstream Republicans as well. Yet, in the thermonuclear heat of the presidential election campaign, the controversy had the unexpected effect of allowing charges of anti-civil sexuality to be plausibly contextualized as expressions of political polarization.

The October revelation about Trump's malevolent misogyny sat between two explosive news investigations that appeared to confirm the connection between ideology, sexual abuse, and media accusation. In July 2016, an investigative journalist at *New York* magazine documented decades of workplace sex abuse by Roger Ailes, the legendary founder and president of the conservative television channel Fox News. The exposé reported on lawsuits that Fox News employees had launched against Ailes, but its traction depended on gumshoe investigation and lengthy, first-time ever interviews. When Ailes was forced to resign in late July, members of the journalist elite hailed it as a professional coup, but also as a victory for journalism's civil ambition. "Journalists are highly competitive, but every once in a while, a reporter is so far out ahead on a continuing story that all the rest of us can do is acknowledge the obvious," the *Washington Post* effused, adding that the ramifications of this high-wire performance went far beyond individual recognition (*WP* 8/2/16). For the first time, journalism was breaking through the wall that insulated workplace sexual abuse from civil evaluation. "Fox News has been notoriously secretive about its inner workings, aggressively managing its public image," the *Post* opined, and the reporter who had broken the story asserted, "now the curtain is fully open and it's incredibly creepy, dark and disturbing" (ibid.).

Combining the personal with the institutional, *New York*'s executive editor joined in: "It's really remarkable what he's done – he's exposed a corporate culture of sexism, harassment and misogyny" (ibid.).

This exposure, however, was taken as a window into the sexual abuse of power at Fox News, not as illuminating a systemic social problem. It was widely interpreted as an attack on right-wing media by a liberal media institution under siege, and this framing seemed only to be confirmed by the *Post*'s anti-Trump revelations three months later during the heat of the campaign. If media exposure of abuse were equated with partisan wrangling, then the possibility of *generalizing* workplace sexual harassment – of attacking it as a broad social problem and of making efforts at civil repair – would be blocked. That polarization blocked societalization was further evidenced the following spring, in April 2017, when the *New York Times* revealed that Fox News had secretly paid out $13 million to protect its immensely influential conservative talk show host, Bill O'Reilly, from sexual harassment charges leveled by female Fox employees (*NYT* 4/1/17). While O'Reilly was forced to resign, the event was reconstructed in a highly partisan manner. To the left, O'Reilly's wrongdoing seemed like an object lesson in right-wing sexual politics. The inverse was true for those on the right, who viewed the exposure of O'Reilly as yet another underhand, distorted leftist political play.

Spread over 10 months, three exposés had breached the wall separating civil from non-civil spheres, repeatedly exposing the social problem of workplace sexual domination. Yet polarization prevented this newly visible social problem from being societalized, from being broadly understood as a deep and systemic danger, one that threatened the premises of the civil sphere itself.

## The Weinstein Exposé Breaks Through

On October 5, 2017 all this changed. The *New York Times* published the results of a year-long investigation into sexual misconduct at the heart of Hollywood (*NYT* 10/5/17) – a geographical location, a factory of globally influential art and fancy, and an ideological confabulation for liberal writers, producers, and actors that conservatives loved to hate. Not only was Harvey Weinstein – the object of the *Times* investigation – the most influential and highly visible mogul in this privileged and powerful world, but he was famously liberal, an activist with close ties, both financial and personal, to leftist causes and leading Democratic politicians. Eight months into the vituperatively anti-liberal Trump presidency, in the midst of furious left-wing resistance, the *Times*' takedown of Weinstein seemed to expose the hypocrisy of preachy and self-righteous liberal ideas. Many conservative commentators jumped on the #MeToo bandwagon, gleefully claiming that liberals had always been among the worst offenders. "The whole 'forgive me, I'm a liberal' thing won't protect him now," wrote conservative *Times*' columnist Ross Douthat; "but it was part of his carapace for decades" (*NYT* 10/7/17). Polemicist Anne Coulter claimed that "the breakthrough of the #MeToo movement was that it was finally acceptable to call out liberal sexual predators. Until recently, it was OK to rape and even murder girls – but only if your name was 'Clinton,' 'Kennedy' or 'Weinstein,' et al." (Breitbart News 9/19/18). Suggesting that "those who shout the loudest are often times the ones most guilty," Glen Beck wrote: "Weinstein brought a nationwide spotlight on something that everyone in Hollywood already knew [but] didn't want out in the public ... until now" (Glennbeck.com 2018). Sean Hannity opined: "It's great what Oprah did by standing up for victims of sexual misconduct and abuse. I think it's awesome. But we can't forget that misconduct is and has been rampant in Hollywood for decades ... There's a lot of hypocrites out there on this specific issue" (Hannity Fox News 2018).

The *Times*' exposé had placed a famously liberal Hollywood mogul in the same boat as Ailes, O'Reilly, and Trump himself, portraying him, if anything, in a more decidedly savage way. But that, of course, was precisely the point. What the four men had in common, the sum of the four media exposés demonstrated, was not their political ideology, but their willingness to put their institutional power at the service of their hunger for sexual domination.[3]

The prize-winning investigation by *Times* reporters Jodi Kantor and Megan Twohey exposed the salacious and corrupt doings of a single, uniquely powerful Hollywood mogul. At the same time, the story represented Weinstein's insidious activities as ideal-typical, as a case study of how elites sustain intrainstitutional control at the expense of the civil sphere. The reporters documented the sexual appetites of a powerful and predatory man, but they also described what happens when civil culture and institutions fail to exercise regulatory control. In the process, Harvey Weinstein became less man than object lesson, his story a parable about the dangers that male sexual desire, rampant still in the postfeminist workplace, posed to civil life. Kantor and Twohey exposed not only sex abuse but, perhaps even more centrally, "abuse of power" (*NYT* 10/5/17) – or, as the *Los Angeles Times* editorialized, how "powerful men still believe they can get away with harassing less powerful women" (*Los Angeles Times* 10/7/17). Kantor and Twohey documented what happens when male lust is uncontrolled by the morality of office and civil obligation. They devoted relatively little attention to the details of Weinstein's sexual predation, but a great deal of attention to how he managed to hide such heinous misconduct from the civil light of day. Their findings were nested inside the critical, judgmental binaries of the civil sphere's moralizing discourse. When Dean Bacquet, *Times*' executive editor, accepted the Pulitzer Prize for public service reporting in the spring of 2018, he represented the newspaper's achievement neither in professional nor in political–ideological terms; instead, employing the language of the civil sphere, he spoke of gender and sexual justice. "By revealing secret settlements, persuading victims to speak and bringing powerful men to account," Bacquet declared, "we spurred a worldwide reckoning about sexual abuse that only seems to be growing" (*NYT* 4/16/18). Bacquet tied journalistic ambition to civil intervention. The *Times*' conscientious commitment to fact and neutrality, its skillful practice of the craft of journalism, had made possible its public service, its civil contribution.

Sexual harassment in the workplace could finally be societalized. The steady state that prevailed for so long inside the Weinstein Company was reconstructed as a cruel, teeming caldron of anti-democratic domination. The man who held financial and managerial power over female workers had asked of women not independence and productivity, but sexual submission. This contrast between women as workers and women as sex objects permeated the *Times*' narrative. The first sentence of the October 5 story began with Weinstein's invitation to actress Ashley Judd to join him at the Peninsula Beverly Hills hotel "for what the young actress expected to be a *business breakfast meeting*" (*NYT* 10/5/17, italics added). Instead, Weinstein "had her sent up to his room where he appeared in a bathrobe and asked if he could give her a massage or she could watch him shower" (ibid.). What followed next was the story of Emily Nestor, "who had worked just one day as a *temporary employee*" before she became subject to Weinstein's depredations (ibid., italics added). Kantor and Twohey assured readers that their report was "documented through interviews with current and former *employees* and film *industry workers*" (ibid., italics added). Weinstein was described as preying on "vulnerable women who hope he will get them *work*" (ibid., italics added). His victims "reported to a hotel for what they thought were *work* reasons" (ibid., italics added). Weinstein's production staff facilitated the transformation of workplace into bedroom. Participating initially in encounters that created a pretense of business, staff would then escort the victims up to Weinstein's private rooms, where he deployed his power to demand sexual submission: "He always came back at me with some new ask ... It was all this ... coercive bargaining" (ibid.).

Weinstein's predatory behavior had been widely known – inside the institution. "Everybody knew." "It wasn't a secret to the inner circle" (*NYT* 11/5/17). "Dozens of Mr. Weinstein's former and current employees, from assistants to top executives, said they knew of inappropriate conduct while they worked for him" (ibid.). Outside the institution, by contrast, virtually nothing was known at all. "From the outside, it seemed golden – the Oscars, the success, the remarkable cultural impact," recounted a former president of Miramax, adding: "but inside it was a mess" (ibid.). The inside mess was insulated by enforcing on victims and staff a "code of silence," English for the *omertà* that the Mafia imposed upon victims, through fear of death (ibid.). The voices of frightened, traumatized, and often very angry women were silenced. Threatened not only with dismissal but with career ruin, they were offered bribes conditional upon the acceptance of non-disclosure agreements (NDAs) that forbade them ever to speak about "the deals or the events that led to them" (ibid.). Film star Asia Argento "did not speak out," the *New Yorker*'s Ronan Farrow attested, "because she feared that Weinstein would 'crush' her" (*New Yorker* 10/10/17). The threat was effective, Argento explained, because "I know he has crushed a lot of people before" (ibid.).

Publicly, Weinstein represented these silencing tactics not as a strategy to hide his sexual domination, but as an effort to maintain institutional equilibrium. "In addressing employee concerns about workplace issues," he told the *Times*, "my motto is to keep the peace" (*NYT* 10/5/17). After being subjected to Weinstein's coercive bargaining, one newly hired female employee sent to company higher-ups a note of bitter complaint: "I remain fearful about speaking up but remaining silent is causing me great distress" (*NYT* 10/5/17). Weinstein and his staff offered her a financial "settlement" that required her to sign an NDA, after which, according to Kantor and Twohey, she "withdrew her complaint and thanked [Weinstein] for the career opportunity he had given her." Weinstein's spokesperson suggested that "the parties made peace very quickly" (ibid.). Rejecting this depiction of a mutually satisfactory steady state, Kantor and Twohey rendered these intrainstitutional interactions as deeply anti-civil, as fundamentally threatening to democracy itself.

The following day a *Los Angeles Times* editorial demanded civil intervention, no matter the intrainstitutional price. It was in part because Weinstein had made so much money and brought so much glory to his company that the board of directors had tolerated and shielded his sexual abuse, at the expense of Weinstein's victims and the larger civil sphere. After code switch, however, the lesson became clear: business "should no longer ignore or tolerate sexual harassment by the powerful against the powerless just because the harassers are making money for them" (*Los Angeles Times* 10/7/17). Another *Los Angeles Times* editorial, three days later, attributed such self-oriented abuse of power to the failure of office regulation: "Weinstein's behavior as described by the women is disgusting, but so are the allegedly widespread efforts on the part of others at his company to cover up for him" (10/11/17). Rather than civil-oriented oversight, those in power had engaged in a cover-up. There had been "collusion," efforts that "concealed" and "enabled," and "the company's entire leadership shares ... blame and shame" (ibid.). Ronan Farrow, who shared a Pulitzer Prize with Kantor and Twohey, described a "culture of complicity" (*New Yorker* 10/10/17).

The *Times* October 5 exposé represented a massive civil intervention. It exploded like a bombshell in the American public sphere, shattering the wall between the civil sphere and the workplace, drawing back the curtain on male sexual behavior, and condemning as deeply anti-democratic what was found inside. Once the code had been switched, the uptake was immediate and the fallout vast. The day of its online publication, ProQuest reported 33 take-ups of the story, across several continents and languages.[4] The next day, when the print version appeared, ProQuest reported 122 take-ups, and 26 other large-circulation print news sources featured reports.[5] Network news programs made it their lead, cable news provided blanket coverage, and blogs turned up the heat 24/7.

One week after the breakout story, on March 15, a television star and activist named Alyssa Milano sent out a twitter message at 4:21 (PDT) in the afternoon. It read:

> Me too. Suggested by a friend: "If all the women who have been sexually harassed or assaulted wrote 'Me too' as a status, we might give people a sense of the magnitude of the problem. If you've been sexually harassed or assaulted, write 'me too' as a reply to this tweet."

By the next morning, Milano had received 55,000 replies, the hashtag trending number 1 on Twitter (*Guardian* 12/1/17). During its first 24 hours, #MeToo was tweeted 110,000 times and spread to Facebook with 12 million posts, comments, and reactions by 4.7 million users worldwide (PR News 10/23/17).[6] Over the next four months, #MeToo tweets averaged 100,000 daily, an academic analyst describing the "constant buzz of

#MeToo tweets" as "the new normal" (Cohen 2018). Before code switch, the social media presence of sexual harassment had been minimal, straightlining for years. After code switch, its social media presence jumped three to four hundred-fold and remained there, with hundreds of thousands mentions daily and millions monthly (*WP* 10/22/18; see Figures 7.1 and 7.2).[7]

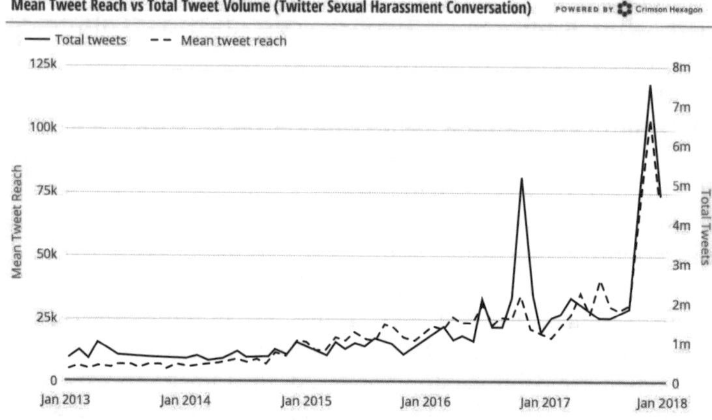


Figure 7.1 Mean Tweet Reach vs Total Tweet Volume (Twitter Sexual Harrassment Conversation)
SOURCE: Crimson Hexagon/George Washington University

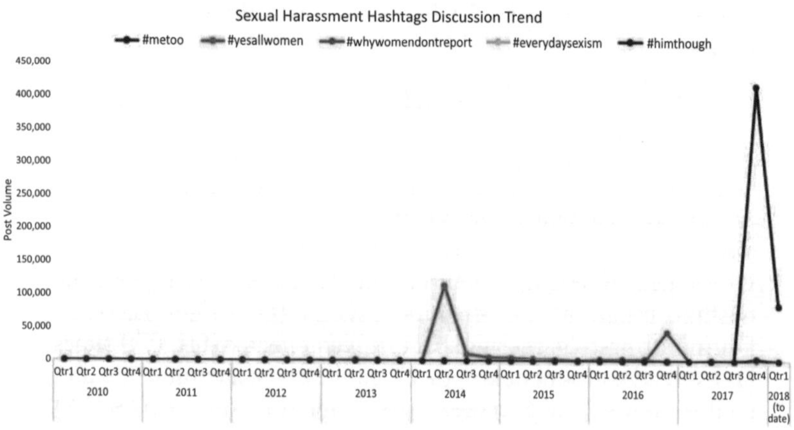


Figure 7.2 Sexual Harrassment Hashtags Discussion Trend
SOURCE: Crimson Hexagon

The hashtag was "meant for the public," a *Washington Post* blogger explained, "a massive show of scale to prove that the issue is unavoidable [and] that its audience is everyone" (*WP* 10/19/17).

Sexual coercion in the workplace had been insulated from the citizen audience, a closely guarded intrainstitutional secret. Now that this "invisible" social problem had become societalized, it felt like a dagger aimed at the heart of the civil sphere itself. Three weeks after the initial revelation, the *Monterey County* [California] *Weekly* (10/26/17) exclaimed: "the floodgates have been opened." Two months later, a contributor to *Bloomberg Businessweek* (12/20/17) observed that "the women who came forward with tales of rape and abuse by Harvey Weinstein set off a cultural earthquake," the "ground is finally shaking," and "it feels at times as if our entire world has started to crumble." Nine months after the initial allegations, in "After #MeToo, the Ripple Effect," the *New York Times* wrote that "nearly every woman seems to have a #MeToo story" (*NYT* 6/28/18).

> One of the most sobering revelations – and one of the most powerful – has been the sheer universality of it … Harassment is pervasive in professions like finance and technology, as well as workplaces like restaurants, factories and hotels. It doesn't spare you if you're old, or rich, or privileged, or powerful. (Ibid.)

## Beyond the Coasts and Elites

In the very midst of this incendiary explosion, however, civil sphere agents, victim activists, and leaders on both left and right wondered repeatedly whether code switch was an illusion, a teapot tempest limited to celebrities and bicoastal elites from which the rest of the country, the "real" America, was left out and unaffected. Sometimes such doubts were ideological, adumbrating a gathering backlash against #MeToo. Often, however, the doubts expressed heartfelt concern that a wider civil solidarity had not been truly engaged.

Whether strategic or sincere, such concerns were off the mark. Certainly, name recognition and the long list of "friends" made up of television and movie stars had greatly enhanced hashtag circulation, but code switch had actually been triggered earlier, by the investigative journalism of the *New York Times*. With deep financial pockets, a massive reportorial staff, and a proud tradition of critical journalism, the *Times* had, for decades, been America's most influential everyday generator of civil judgment, and more recently perhaps the global civil sphere's as well. With 1 million print readers and 2 million unique digital subscribers, its news reporting set the national agenda of the day, for newspapers and also for television, radio, and social media.[8] The Kantor–Twohey story triggered a massive circulation of civil grievance that social media subsequently intensified, expanding social solidarity throughout the American civil sphere, among groups and individuals otherwise separated by religion, region, and class.

*Religion*

On October 19, the *New Jersey Jewish News* (10/19/17) reported on the "furious backlash" among Orthodox Jewish women against an orthodox male leader's widely publicized advice to Jewish women that they wear modest clothing to protect themselves against sexual harassment. Blaming the victim like this, the women complained, ignored the "Weinstein-like behavior" of orthodox men – in the workplace, on dates, and on the street (ibid.). The angry responders drew a parallel between "male-dominated" Hollywood and the "rigid hierarchy and patriarchal structure" of the Orthodox Jewish community (ibid.). They found the same "code of silence … in insular religious circles," one that allowed "seemingly pious men [to] have free and unfettered rein" to commit "aggression" against powerless and constrained women (ibid.).

Two months later, the *Jacksonville Free Press* (12/7/17), described on its masthead as "Florida's First Coast Quality Black Weekly," wrote about women using "the #churchtoo hashtag to shed light on countless disturbing experiences" "Hundreds of women," the newspaper reported, "have been revealing stories of rape, sexual abuse, and harassment that they suffered inside church or at the hands of Christian men in leadership" (ibid.). One churchgoing woman complained:

> I CANNOT COUNT the number of times I've heard guys in church PUBLICLY admit to molestation, harassment, assault, etc., only to be praised for their bravery and honesty. No consequences. The church's legacy of protecting abusers is sickening. (Ibid.)

*Region*

On October 17, under the headline "Houston Women Join #MeToo Movement," the website of KHOU 11, a leading local news radio, reported that "women from all over the country are joining forces to speak out against sexual abuse [and] now hundreds here in Houston are doing the same" (KHOU 11 10/17/17). A week later, Connecticut's *Hartford Courant* headlined "#All of Us: Why #MeToo Is Taking Off" (10/22/17). Suggesting that "the case of Harvey Weinstein [has] resonated in a moving and profound way with women across the state and the nation," the state's leading newspaper published responses to its Facebook appeal that readers "tell us why #metoo took off and what they hoped it would achieve" (ibid.). Laura Mahon from Tolland, CT, asked: "Is there a woman out there who has NOT been harassed/ assaulted?" (ibid.). Lucy Ferriss from West Hartford, saying "so much has led up to this," eloquently enumerated

> the pat on the fanny by the senior manager; the inappropriate familiarity of the HS [high school] teacher; the coercive boyfriend; the stranger in the deserted subway who exposes himself; the boss who offers a promotion but only in exchange for sex; the boss who threatens firing if you don't have sex; the doctor who gropes; the date rapist; the violent husband; the violent rapist,

then concluded: "None of it is OK anymore … Women have been pushed too far, gotta push back hard" (ibid.). From Jill Fletcher in Wethersfield: "At last something pushed through the seemingly impenetrable. #MeToo creates an avalanche of solidarity for all the hurts that have been buried and resonates … It took many voices to actually break through" (ibid.). From Marianne O'Hare in Stonington: "Weinstein et al. are merely the top of the pyramid. I think the greatest tragedies occur systematically as we go down that pyramid to women who have no power at all" (ibid.).

Days later, the *Santa Barbara Independent*, headlining "Schools on #MeToo Track" (10/26/17), reported that "high school girls [are] increasingly concerned with sex crimes and misconduct." In early November, the *Colorado Springs Independent* (11/8/17a) headlined "The Profound Prevalence," bemoaning that workplace sexual harassment had become so "pedestrian that it no longer stands out when it happens." Later that month, an anonymous contributor to the *Miami Times* (11/19/17) warned: "We in Miami should not get on our high horses and proclaim this as a problem of the Washington Beltway or the entertainment capitals of Los Angeles and New York" – predicting that "#MeToo will show up in sunny South Florida." Four months after that, in March 2018, the *Atlanta Journal Constitution* (3/16/18) published another installment from its months-long investigation into sexual harassment in Georgia's state government. Noting that Georgia's capital was "largely run by men," one of the American South's most influential newspapers reported that an "imbalance of power" had created a "cesspool of misogyny." The investigation documented how "the public is kept from knowing [the] misdeeds of their elected officials" and described how "complaints are handled behind closed doors by a small group of lawmakers whose processes are unknown" (ibid.)

*Class*

On October 16, under the headline "#MeToo Brings Dallas Stories of Sexual Assault to Social Media," the *Dallas News* printed the story of "Liz Landry's first job at a grocery store," which "became a nightmare when the morning a manager came up from behind and pressed his pelvis against her, massaging her shoulders":

> At 19, she didn't feel she could bring legal charges in the mostly male corporate environment of the 1990s. Today, the 38-year-old who works as an advocate for those affected by sexual abuse in Dallas used #MeToo to speak out on that long-ago incident. (*Dallas News* 10/16/17)

Early the next month, the *Colorado Springs Independent* (11/8/17b) published a first-hand testimonial under the headline "#WhoHasn't."

> I was 22 years old. I was a waitress at a popular downtown restaurant and had finished my shift. I decided to stick around and listen to the band that was playing for the Halloween weekend. One of our regulars, a banker, came up and put his hand on my ass and said something like, "This is a great pumpkin you've got here." He kept his hand right there, squeezing. I turned to him and said, "Take your hand off my ass, they're not paying me to let you do this..." Of course, I could have walked into the managers' office and reported things, right? Oh sure, the office where they had a photocopied sign pinned on the corkboard that read, "Sexual harassment will not be tolerated here, but it will be graded." What would I have said? "Surprise grab, firm grasp, cheesy line? C+ at best." No, I didn't say anything and I'm sure I waited on the same man more times with a smile on my face.

"Until Celebrities Said 'me too,' Nobody Listened to Blue-Collar Women about Assault," headlined the *Chicago Sun Times* in March 2018, over an op-ed by an anti-harassment activist. The author, a labor attorney, argued that #MeToo had shed an "overdue spotlight on workplace sexual violence ... in blue collar industries" (*Chicago Sun Times* 3/21/28), reporting that one working-class woman told her: "Finally! It's not just us – it happens to rich people too." In September 2018, the *Guardian* devoted a story to "the protest and outcry of ordinary women" (9/18/18).

> Last Tuesday, McDonald's workers in 10 US cities walked off the job to protest against pervasive sexual harassment. A week earlier, female janitors in California marched 100 miles from San Francisco to the state capitol in Sacramento to support anti-harassment legislation. The janitors' union, SEIU, in partnership with the East LA Women's Center, has been quietly training women in self-defense and promoting peer-to-peer anti-harassment workshops and an assault crisis hotline. (Ibid.; cf. *NYT* 9/19/18)

## Civil Repair as Culture (Re-)Structure

The first and perhaps still most significant civil repair that societalization effected was to create a new set of social meanings. A radically altered culture structure emerged, a public, sharply critical but also emancipatory collective representation of sexual harassment in the workplace and of the struggle against it. The abstract ethical binaries marking civil sacred and profane now became specified in a gender-inverted way. Sexually aggressive men came to be seen as untrustworthy, secretive, dishonest, and anti-civil and their female victims as trustworthy, open, honest, and civil. These newly resignified characters became protagonists and antagonists in a liberation narrative about defeating oppression and creating justice in the workplace. Men, once admired as macho heroes in the battle of the sexes, became vilified as perpetrators. Women, once depicted as weak and helpless, were now hailed as heroines whose courage and bravery were praised for example by serial celebrities in the *Washington Post* (*WP* 10/13/17), six days after the Weinstein revelations.

> "It's wonderful they have this incredible courage and are standing up now." (Matt Damon)
> "Their bravery in speaking out." (Gretchen Mol)
> "Their bravery to come forward." (Jennifer Lawrence)
> "The intrepid women who raised their voices to expose this abuse." (Meryl Streep)
> "Incredibly brave." (Kate Winslett)
> "Forever in awe of the bravery of those who spoke out." (Lin-Manuel Miranda)

With the code shifted and an emancipatory narrative in place, aggrieved women who cried foul and pointed fingers were accorded a new civil status, one that allowed them to become respected narrators of their own social suffering. "Telling their own stories" was the red thread that ran through the many months and tens of thousands of #MeToo testimonies. "The story isn't that Mr. Weinstein has been fired," wrote Gretchen Carlson, Roger Ailes' former accuser, in the *New York Times* on October 10, but "that women's voices are finally being heard" (*NYT* 10/10/17). Six days later, the once abused grocery clerk turned sexual abuse advocate declared to the *Dallas News* (10/16/17): "telling your story is powerful [because] talking about it is the only way we start creating what it looks like." Half a year later, an ethicist at Barron's, the business magazine, reiterated the argument in a more analytical way:

> Women ... have had the opportunity to tell their stories. Part of what is happening as a result of this movement is a re-imagining of the boundaries ... Unwelcome sexual comments and physical attentions previously dismissed as "boys being boys" or "locker-room talk" have been redefined as harassment. Women whose accounts were belittled or trivialized now have the space to reclaim their narrative. (Barron's 4/24/18)

*Time* magazine awarded its 2017 Person of the Year award to the "Silence Breakers" (*Time* 12/18/17).

Women telling personal stories about sexual abuse had become serious public business. Such performances of civil indignation projected not only deep pain, but authenticity, and they were widely believed. Audiences in the civil sphere listened carefully and often reported piercing experiences of emotional identification, seeing in such stories not just the victims but themselves, and their friends and family members too. Empathy extended, solidarity deepened, and civil feeling stretched not only to other women but also to men, who contributed 37 percent of the tweets during the first three and a half months of #MeToo (Cohen 2018). A 41-year-old Dallas resident named Marty Yudizky wrote that, while "I have not personally been a victim of sex assault," he was tweeting "to show solidarity and compassion with the women posting 'metoo'" (Dallas News 10/16/17). After tweeting about her own abuse experiences, a Colorado woman posted: "I witnessed the reaction of male friends discovering their eighth of eight female relatives had posted these two words. I saw another male friend's breakdown when he found that post [#MeToo] on his sister's page. It was powerful – too powerful" (*Colorado Springs Independent* 11/8/17a).

"Her story" was not just hers, not just a personal account, but something that had the ring of a broader truth, about power and trauma – and survival. Indeed, women telling their #MeToo stories were accorded the sacred status of "survivor." According to post-Holocaust morality (Alexander 2003), being a survivor provided precious authenticity, allowing personal testimony to be taken as moral truth.

## Material Regulation

Societalization had barely commenced when activists and critics began wringing their hands that nothing was really going to change. These worries took the form of a binary that expressed itself in such contrasts as talk versus action, soft versus hard, feeling versus structure, individual versus system, and belief versus organization. On October 16, just one day after the hashtag began circulating, at the very center of the gathering firestorm, a postdoctoral fellow in Vancouver posted, "I don't think #MeToo signals some kind of 'watershed moment,'" but "I am hoping that it serves as another link in the chain to some concrete, systemic change" (*WP* 10/16/17). After three months of societalization, a *Washington Post* contributor declared that "the #MeToo movement will be in vain if we don't make … changes [in] our legal system" and that "without substantial reforms [the] movement may be all for naught" (*WP* 1/25/18). On the six-month anniversary of her and Twohey's code-shifting *New York Times* investigation, Jodi Kantor crystalized these fears in a deeply pessimistic survey and retrospective. While she acknowledged that "the #MeToo moment" had "shifted social attitudes" and "resulted in unprecedented accountability," Kantor rued that there had merely been "revelations about the pervasiveness of harassment" but nothing systemic and structural – no "legal and institutional" measures to prevent or punish it (*NYT* 3/24/18).

Those who are in the midst of a radical social change often fail to understand it. Their restless energy is devoted to making things happen, more stuff and faster, not to looking back on what may already have changed. Inside the messy contingency of protest, it is hard to see the forest for the trees. Those with less of a stake in the struggle can sometimes be more reflexive, recognizing that the forest itself has been changed. One month after Kantor's anxiety and regret, on April 19, 2018, *The American Conservative* got it much more right: "It's six months since #MeToo began trending on social media. Since then these two little words have sparked a conversation about sexual harassment in work that has spread across the globe and into every walk of life"

(*The American Conservative* 4/19/2018). Societalization had produced new cultural understandings that were structural, systemic, and collective. These shifted the course of social action. But there was more; for, when ideas change, materiality often follows.

## Toppling Elite Males

The most visible material effect of code switch was the physical inversion of gender power, the objective destruction of the careers of hundreds of rich and powerful men who composed the intrainstitutional elite. The aroused civil sphere, having resignified these men as abusive perpetrators, entered into their institutions and forced them to leave. This material effect did not take place via police action; few accused perpetrators were arrested, and none has yet gone to jail. What happened was more like a citizen's arrest. A new phase of the gender revolution was being effected, and it was time to *couper le tête de la* (male) *bourgeoisie*: "Another Executive's Head Rolls at Besieged CBS" (*NYT* 9/13/18a). Taking stock of #MeToo after one year, *Times* journalists found that, despite a "crackling backlash," the movement had shaken, and was "still shaking," the "power structures in society's most visible sectors" and that, as a result, the "corridors of power" had been remarkably changed (*NYT* 10/23/18). "After public allegations of sexual harassment," more than 200 extraordinarily "prominent" men had lost their jobs, and nearly half had been replaced by women (ibid.). It was not only that the civil sphere had entered into the workplace and ejected anti-civil men from power; it was that a form of power now construed as more civil – female power – had taken its place. "Research has repeatedly shown," the *Times* reported, "that women tend to lead differently [by] creat[ing] more respectful work environments, where harassment is less likely to flourish and where women feel more comfortable reporting it" (ibid.). In the corporate world, women managers "hire and promote more women" and "pay them more equally." In government, "women have been shown to be more collaborative and bipartisan" (ibid.). A law professor from Hastings College at the University of California interpreted the gender transformation of power in terms of contrasting risks: "Women had always been seen as risky, because they might do something like have a baby. But men are now being seen as more risky hires" – because of what was now construed as their anti-civil proclivity for sexual domination (ibid.). With societalization, women "are starting to gain power in organizations," with "potentially far-reaching," and decidedly civilizing, effects (ibid.).[9]

## Reconstructing Organizational Insides

Analyzing the societalization of the financial crisis earlier in this book, I observed that, long before new government regulations went into effect, Wall Street firms hired compliance officers to reconstruct their investment strategies in more civil ways – not necessarily because they agreed with external demands for civil repair but because they hoped to avoid the material costs of seeming to violate them. The same kind of self-restructuring marked the behavior of major corporations in the wake of #MeToo, which had "touched almost every industry" (PEW Stateline 7/31/18). If the United States had become "a vastly different country with sharply different values," as the *Los Angeles Times* (9/17/18) contended, such that "the public's definition of what constitutes acceptable [sexual] conduct" had been deeply changed (ibid.), then organizations whose material interests depended on staying right with public opinion would themselves have to change.

The *New York Times* reported that, in the wake of #MeToo, companies felt they were exposed to "a serious reputational and business risk" (*NYT* 3/24/18) and that, in response, a "fear-driven shift" in intrainstitutional policies had begun (cf. Market Watch 7/14/18). Corporate boards, managers, and investors "from Wall Street to Silicon Valley are going on the offensive, probing for problems to avoid being surprised" (*NYT* 3/24/18). Shareholders tried to ascertain whether or not companies had instituted appropriate anti-harassment controls. "While sexual violence in the workplace endangers those who endured it," Market Watch (2/16/18) reported, it "might make the predators' companies a bad investment too." Cornerstone Capital, an investment advisory and wealth management firm, employed the discourse of the civil sphere to measure the capacity for profitability. Warning prospective investors against "structural complicity" with harassers, the firm declared "sexual and gender-based violence" to be an "emerging investment risk" (ibid.), concluding that "it is incumbent upon investors to demand greater transparency on issues of SGBV – to hold companies accountable." If capital markets did not hold companies to such civil standards, then, according to the advisory firm, companies would be regarded as "complicit" in abuse (ibid.). The outplacement and executive coaching firm Challenger, Gray & Christmas (2018) urged employers "to get ahead of potential problems" and to become "more aware of power dynamics" (ibid.). Fortune quoted a University of New Haven expert on workplace romance who suggested: "the underlying message of top management must be that their workplace is one of civility where employees get by on their merits" (Fortune 7/18/18).

*Forbes* magazine analyzed what had gone wrong at CBS, the television and entertainment company that had been hugely embarrassed by a series of accusations and forced departures in the months after code switch. CBS's board had been "far too detached and passive," *Forbes* (9/17/18) reported, suggesting that "an independent internal investigation" had been far too late responding to what the *New York Times* (9/13/18b) characterized as "deceit" on the part of Les Moonves, CBS chair and CEO. The CBS board "was too slow to be transparent," agreed the female CEO of the Santa Fe Group (ibid.).

Reporting on a survey of 150 human resources executives, Workforce found that "HR departments [were] stepping up their responses," hiring outside contractors to "perform workplace culture audits," providing "independent whistleblower services," and "increasing sexual harassment training" in house (Workforce 4/3/18). The founder of the field of sexual harassment training testified: "I would be booked between now and 10 years ... and still not fulfill the demand" (*NYT* 3/23/18). According to business cable channel CNBC, companies were turning to private investigators "to identify predators," not only inside their own institutions but inside their rivals' as well; such a practice of "weaponizing feminism" often involved "massive intrusions into businessmen's private lives" (CNBC 5/31/18).

Advertising agencies dramatically revised employee dating policies (*Digiday* 2/5/18). After 20,000 Google employees walked off their jobs to protest the company's handling of sex harassment complaints, the tech giant announced it would no longer force employees to accept private arbitration of such claims. The next day Facebook did the same (*NYT* 11/9/18). Microsoft had changed its arbitration policy a year before, eliminated forced arbitration agreements (FAAs), and began lobbying for similar changes in federal law (Fortune 12/19/17). After UBER ended forced arbitration, it hired former Attorney General Eric Holder's law firm to conduct a wide-ranging internal examination (*Time* 2/21/17). Conde Nast announced new rules about "nudity and touching" (*NYT* 10/23/17).

Barron's featured an influential business ethics expert responding to "knotty questions from people in the advisory industry." (Barron's 4/24/18):

> I am the leader of a large practice [and] recently held a team-building event for my financial advisors and administrative support staff. At this event, one of the top producers, a male in his early 50s, was overheard making several jokes about the "#MeToo" movement ... Several people witnessed this and were offended by the remarks ... I'm not sure of the best way to respond now.

The ethicist responded that, "as a leader, you should immediately bring the team together" and make clear that "the conversation mocking the #MeToo movement violated" company values, that it was "harmful to the organization," and that "people who violate these values will not be permitted to harm the cohesion of the unit." Stressing it was important "to take a strong tone," she advised the executive to "meet with the 'ringleader' alone, and ask him if he agrees with what you've said" to the group. "If he agrees," then you "can ask for his support," in which case he may become "an influencer within the organization." If, however, the ringleader "is non-committal," then "you have an important decision to make," for it has then become "a decision about who will dictate the culture of the firm – him or you."

## Gaining Legal Traction

In the midst of societalization, the conviction was continually expressed that sexual harassment in the workplace was rampant because laws to prevent it had not been put in place, and that civil repair would need to center on legal reform. Quite the opposite, however, was actually the case. Already in 1964, the Civil Rights Act had established a powerful foundation for constructing anti-harassment law, and in 1980 the Equal Employment Opportunity Commission (EEOC) declared specifically that workplace sexual harassment violated Title VII, which prohibited harassment based on sex, race, and national origin (*WP* 1/25/18). In 1986, the Supreme Court ruled that hostile work environments also violated Title VII, and in 1991 Congress made compensatory and punitive damages available under Title VII as well. During these decades and after, a thick web of sex discrimination law developed (ibid.; cf. *Time* 4/11/16 and Siegel 2003).

Strong legal protections were in place before the societalization of sexual harassment began. Here is the policy of the EEOC, which defined normative workplace behavior and prosecuted departures from it:

> It is unlawful to harass a person (an applicant or employee) because of that person's sex. Harassment can include "sexual harassment" or unwelcome sexual advances, requests for sexual favors, and other verbal or physical harassment of a sexual nature [if] it is so frequent or severe that it creates a hostile or offensive work environment or when it results in an adverse employment decision (such as the victim being fired or demoted). (US Equal Employment Opportunity Commission n.d.)

In early January 2018, a powerful Florida law firm specializing in employee rights noted that it had "been a long road [making] sexual harassment illegal in the workplace," and listed 16 critical legal decisions between 1964 and 2005. Declaring "there are laws that are now in place to help protect employees from unwanted sexual advances and conduct of a sexual nature that can affect their ability to do their job," the firm assured prospective clients, "if you've been a victim of sexual harassment and/or wrongfully terminated or retaliated against for reporting sexual harassment, you are protected under federal and state laws" (Wenzel Fenton Cabassa, P.A. 1/1/18).

What, then, was the problem? Why had sexual harassment in the workplace continued, relatively unabated, during the same period as such a legal network emerged? Laws are external constraints on action; they must be activated internally, by will and imagination, and this happens only if legal regulation is connected with a shared cultural core. Energizing such a core is what code switch is all about. Four months after societalization began, Catharine MacKinnon, the pioneering feminist legal scholar whose decades of work helped build the legal lattice against sexual harassment, declared in a *New York Times* op-ed that "the #MeToo movement is accomplishing what sexual harassment law to date has not" (*NYT* 4/4/18). The "disbelief and trivializing dehumanization of its victims," MacKinnon wrote – the "denial by abusers and devaluing of accusers" – had long prevented sexual harassment law from having a significant effect (ibid.). Because women's "complaints were routinely passed off with some version of 'she wasn't credible' or 'she wanted it,'" many "survivors realistically judged reporting pointless" (ibid.). While "it is widely thought that when something is legally prohibited, it more or less stops," MacKinnon warned, that is anything but the case; certainly, "it is not true for pervasive practices like sexual harassment" (ibid.). It is "cultural inequalities" that count, and they can be broken only when "publicly and pervasively challenged by women's voices" (ibid.).

> No longer liars, no longer worthless, today's survivors are initiating consequences none of them could have gotten through any lawsuit ... They are being believed and valued as the law seldom has. Women have been saying these things forever. It is the response to them that has changed. (Ibid.)

Men who harassed women had been resignified. There is now a "revulsion against harassing behavior" and "men with power [are] refusing to be associated with it" (ibid.). Women's stories, now seen as authentic, are fusing with citizen audiences. When these storytellers identify male behavior as predatory and polluted, those listening and looking, including many men, see it that way too. Laws are essential to maintaining civil behavior and extending solidarity, but such regulative power must be communicatively intertwined. Only if anti-harassment laws are infused with social meaning will they be able to exercise regulative power.

None of this meant that anti-harassment law could not be strengthened. Indeed, the prospect of existing law finally gaining traction made contemporary gaps and lacunae more evident. If egregious episodes of earlier harassment were to be prosecuted, statutes of limitations would have to be lifted. For victims to speak more freely, non-disclosure agreements should have to be scrutinized and eliminated. Forced arbitration could be neutralized, and private litigations costs underwritten to neutralize upfront attorney fees. Monetary caps on pain and suffering might be raised. Should companies be required to report harassment claims to the federal government, for example, as part of the Labor Department's annual Survey of Occupational Injuries and Illnesses? In the interests of fairness, should legislation address the issue of proportionate punishment for different levels of severity (PEW Stateline 7/31/18, BillTrack50 2/15/18, *WP* 1/25/18)? In the first five months of 2018, according to the National Conference of State Legislators, 32 states introduced over 125 different pieces of legislation, "an unprecedented amount of legislation on sexual harassment and sexual harassment policies" (National Conference of State Legislatures 6/6/18). By the year's end, many of these bills had been signed into law, in such high-population centers as New York state, New York City, California, Illinois, and Maryland – but in states such as Vermont, Maine, Delaware, Connecticut, and New Mexico as well (*Real Estate in Depth* 10/18, Pillsbury Insights 10/8/18, Winston & Strawn LLP 6/14/18).

## Backlash

The societalization of workplace sexual harassment had unfolded in the midst of one of the most poisonously polarized political periods in living memory. It was during the second year of Donald Trump's administration that women and men were resignified; that women were accepted as authentic narrators of their own stories; that citizen audiences identified with their trauma, expressing a revulsion that destroyed the careers of powerful men and put women in their place, restructuring the internal environments of institutions and allowing anti-harassment law to gain more traction. Sexual harassment in the workplace became societalized because it could be constructed, not as a matter of political right or left, but rather as a problem of society itself. That men shared in this newly extended solidarity was symbolized by the performance of public apology. Many accused men engaged in such performances, even when these were tepid – starting with Harvey Weinstein himself: "I appreciate the way I've behaved with colleagues in the past has caused a lot of pain and I sincerely apologize for it. Though I'm trying to do better, I know I have a long way to go" (*NYT* 10/5/17).

Despite such reintegration and repair, however – indeed, precisely because of it – societalization triggers backlash. #MeToo sparked resistance among members of the male elite, but for many months such pushback did not express itself in a politicized, right versus left way. Running just below the visible surface of apologetic rituals of degradation, for example, there were rivulets of resentment. Even as the public narrative of accusation, punishment, repentance, and restructuring became hegemonic, the majority of men who were exposed and humiliated failed to publicly accept responsibility. A rough survey between October 5, 2017, and May 23, 2018 reveals that, while some 40 percent did stage an apologetic performance, 60 percent did not apologize, not even tepidly.[10]

Pushback against civil intrusion into workplace sexuality actually began before societalization, when code shift was only a distant possibility. When communicative agents of the civil sphere began investigating the sexual behavior of men who held key institutional positions, members of the male elite deployed their power in an effort to prevent news stories from being written and published. In February 2017, as *New York Times*' reporter Emily Steel worked her way into the contentious issues at Fox News, Bill O'Reilly called, telling her, on the record, "I am coming after you with everything

I have" and "you can take it as a threat" (*NYT* 10/15/17). When the *Times* began sleuthing into the intrainstitutional behavior of Harvey Weinstein, Jodi Kantor recounted, the Hollywood mogul threatened to sue the newspaper – "he had one high-priced consultant or lawyer after another" (*WP* 1/25/18); Megan Twohey, her co-author, recalls "an army – it was an army attacking us" (ibid.). When a CBS News reporter asked Jeff Fager, the powerful executive producer of *60 Minutes*, to respond to harassment accusations leveled against him, he warned her to "be careful," threatening "there are people who lost their jobs trying to harm me, and if you pass on these damaging claims without … reporting to back them up that will become a serious problem" (*NYT* 9/13/18). "They throw up as many hurdles as possible [and] many used threats," recalled the *Times* editor who had supervised the paper's investigation into sexual harassment in Silicon Valley (*NYT* 10/15/17).

As published investigations began intruding into the workplace, many of the men exposed as male predators, despite performances of apology, professed to disbelieve many particulars of the exposés. "I don't know anything about that," Weinstein responded to the *Times* account of his years-long harassment of a long-time employee (*NYT* 10/7/17). Investigating how "#MeToo has changed the DC power structure," the *Washington Post* reported that, among the 19 powerful political figures who had been forced from office, "the majority were defiant, accusing women of lying" (*WP* 9/26/18). Supporters of stigmatized men often pushed back as well. Responding to explosive charges against CBS chair and CEO Les Moonves – accusations that eventually drove him from office – board of directors member Arnold Kopelson, the 83-year-old movie producer who had won an Oscar for *Platoon*, pledged institutional loyalty: "I don't care if 30 more women come forward and allege this kind of stuff, Les is our leader and it wouldn't change my opinion of him" (*NYT* 9/13/18b: A1).

As the #MeToo crisis deepened and societalization gained tsunami strength, isolated acts of resistance began to be stitched together, forming a "rhetoric of reaction" (Hirschman 1991) that, while circulating mostly on right-wing websites and Fox News, created a profile on the public scene. The civil sphere remained central to this backlash discourse, but its relation to #MeToo was radically changed. Rather than expanding civil solidarity, the societalization of sexual harassment was here construed as endangering it. Backlash challenged the truth-telling status of female victims. "Women should not be reflexively believed," one Breitbart critic wrote (Breitbart News 2/14/18). Because "facts have been readily sacrificed for the good of the cause," we should no longer "automatically take woman's words as the truth" (*The American Conservative* 4/19/18). "I don't believe a word of it," the famous fashion designer Karl Lagerfeld proclaimed, adding "if you don't want your pants pulled about, don't become a model! Join a nunnery, there'll always be a place for you in the convent" (*Numéro* 4/12/18). The rising force of anti-harassment public opinion was attacked as a form of mass hysteria, as "a mob mentality" that had left reason aside (Breitbart News 2/14/18). #MeToo was "driven by the mainstream media that is calling for public stoning" (ibid.). "Infantile and authoritarian" (*The American Conservative* 4/19/18), #MeToo had become had a "witch hunt" that smacked of "McCarthyism" (RedState Blog 11/29/17). A French petition of protest, signed by 100 leading female figures in the arts and entertainment, blamed #MeToo for trying to create a "climate of totalitarianism":

> We are all being told what is proper to say ... Women [are] enslave[d] to a status of eternal victim [and those] who refuse to fall in line are considered traitors. [There are] public confessions. (*NYT* 1/9/18)

Despite its libertine animus, this French protest was eagerly taken up by the emerging backlash line (e.g. *The American Conservative* 4/19/18).

"#HimToo" soon popped up as a hashtag (*NYT* 12/14/17). Declaring that "tropes of predatory men and vulnerable women are outdated" (*The American Conservative* 4/19/18), backlash turned the #MeToo narrative upside down. Women making accusations were now described as predators, and men the victims – of women's false accusations. Complaining that "the current climate" had led "many men to resent and be angry toward women," Andrew Yarrow claimed #MeToo "hinders teamwork" (*Forbes* 9/17/18). Fox News senior analyst Brit Hume tweeted: "Mike Pence's policy of avoiding being alone with women other than his wife looking better every day" (*Newsweek* 11/17/17). "Men are going to be afraid of working with women," Breitbart News (2/14/18) warned. "Male managers ... have grown significantly more uncomfortable mentoring women than before," LeanIn.org reported (*USA Today* 10/8/18).

According to such "rhetoric of reaction," the civil sphere had to be protected from #MeToo if democracy were to survive. Newly emergent cultural structures were anti-democratic; they must be avoided and, if possible, destroyed. Female subjectivity could not be trusted. Women were abusing men. #MeToo women were dangerously anti-civil, making use of corrupt communicative institutions to conduct witch hunts. To protect themselves, victimized males would need to rely on other civil sphere institutions, especially the law. Only due process – the fair, balanced, and objective evaluation of material evidence in a court of law – could protect men's democratic rights (*The American Conservative* 4/19/18, Breitbart News 2/14/18). Unless there was "proof" – in the quasi-scientific sense – male guilt could not be proclaimed. In lieu of such legal documentation, women's stories didn't matter, their voices would be silenced, their truth denied, and their invidiousness, not their authenticity, proclaimed.

It was with this gradually congealing rhetoric of reaction that the confrontation between Judge Brett Kavanaugh and Dr. Christine Blasey Ford collided in the late summer of 2018. Conservative ideologues had chipped away at the new culture structure of societalization, yet they had not managed to make their backlash construction ideologically important to the nation's ongoing left–right polarization. President Trump, for example, had barely been mentioned throughout the many months of gender confrontation; neither he nor the conservative movement had been objects of #MeToo. When Blasey Ford accused her youthful acquaintance Brett Kavanaugh of having sexually abused her at a high school party, however, everything changed. President Trump had nominated Kavanaugh to the Supreme Court, an appointment that, if confirmed by the Senate, would help ensure a conservative majority for decades to come. With the help of liberal Democratic Senator Dianne Feinstein, Ford publicly launched her accusation just days before Kavanaugh's nomination was to have come up for a vote in the Republican-controlled Senate Judiciary Committee, where support for confirmation had seemed assured. Ford's claim that Kavanaugh had tried to rape her exploded as a "#MeToo moment;" with the winds of societalization at its back, the accusation threatened to upend Kavanaugh's confirmation and undermine an imminent conservative triumph. President Trump became enraged, as did most Republican senators and conservatives throughout the nation.

Sexually abused women had overcome marginalization, and the societalization of their plight had managed largely to escape the invidious effects of contemporary polarization. This generalized status was now being torn away. "The movement originally founded to help victims has become weaponized as a political tool," the conservative blog Red State exclaimed in late September 2018 (RedState Blog 9/24/18). "For many conservatives, especially white men who share Mr. Trump's contempt for the left and his use of divisive remarks," the *Times* reported on the eve of the Senate hearings, "the clash over Judge Kavanaugh's confirmation has become a rallying cry against a liberal order that, they argue, is hostile to their individual rights, political power and social status" (*NYT* 9/30a/18: A23). That same day, from the other side of the political chasm, a female member of the *Times* editorial staff, in a signed editorial "What America Owes Women," reminded Americans that "Dr. Blasey said she shared her story out of a sense of civic duty," and asserted "now it's up to the men of this country to hear us," that this "is what we are owed, as citizens and as human beings" (*NYT* 9/30d/18: SR8). Would #MeToo become identified with leftist critique rather than with systemic social problems? If so, then the societalization of sexual harassment would be blocked and incomplete.

In a front-page story headlined "Fight over Kavanaugh Shows the Power, and Limits, of #MeToo," the *Times* suggested that "the fight over [Kavanaugh's] nomination shows how the dynamics of the #MeToo movement have threaded their way into American life" (*NYT* 9/30b/18: A1a). Twenty years earlier, the all-male Senate Judiciary Committee had greeted with demeaning incredulity Anita

Hill's charges of sexual harassment against Supreme Court nominee Clarence Thomas. Now, in sharp contrast, even most conservative senators went out of their way to exhibit elaborate courtesy to Kavanaugh's accuser, exercising great care not to appear publicly to challenge her story, allowing that it was her "truth." The Republican chair of the Judiciary Committee put off the date of Ford's required appearance, acceding to her request for more time for preparation. When the hearings actually unfolded, the Republican side's questioning of Dr. Blasey was handled by a Deputy County Attorney from Arizona, an expert on sex crimes whom they had hired for the occasion – to avoid any appearance of male bullying and domination.

Despite these efforts to prevent Kavanaugh's Senate confirmation from becoming ensnared by societalization, the hearing became "an explosive collision between #MeToo – the cultural movement shaking the country – and the politics of outrage that drive President Trump's Republican Party" (*NYT* 9/27/18). Ford's tearful recounting of her sexual harassment appeared authentic, a moving representation of #MeToo coding and narration. Kavanaugh's testimony was represented, by mainstream media, as an angry, bitter, and accusatory response from the backlash side.

> Republicans [had] outsourced their questioning of Dr. Blasey to a female lawyer because they worried about the optics of an all-male panel quizzing a woman about sensitive matters. But by the time they got to Judge Kavanaugh, Republicans could no longer hold their tongues. They treated him as a victim, treated unfairly by a society eager to be sympathetic to women's allegations. In a tirade, Senator Lindsey Graham, Republican of South Carolina, called the accusations '"crap" and "the most despicable thing" he'd seen in his time in politics. (Ibid.)

The Republican majority on the Judiciary Committee approved Kavanaugh's nomination, and their Senate majority soon confirmed it. When he swore Kavanaugh into office on October 8, the president pointedly apologized to him and his family "for the terrible pain and suffering *you* have been forced to endure" (*NYT* 10/24/18, italics added).

Republicans won the battle, but they may have lost the war. Forty days after 11 Republican senators on the Judiciary Committee voted to approve Kavanaugh, some 113 million Americans entered voting booths to participate in the biannual, nation-wide Congressional elections. Trump had tried making the election turn on *Ford v. Kavanaugh*, hoping the conservative Senate victory had so stoked the backlash against #MeToo that it would neutralize the Democratic "blue wave" threatening Republican control of the House of Representatives. "For a while," the *Times* reported, the president "said that 'this will be an election of Kavanaugh, the [immigrant] caravan, law and order, and common sense'" (*NYT* 11/7/18). For a while, perhaps, but soon the president had stopped. "Kavanaugh" was not a winning hand. A majority of Americans told pollsters that they sympathized with Blasey Ford, not Kavanaugh, believing her story, not the recollection of the judge (NPR 10/3/18). Far from fueling Republican electoral victory, the Senate confrontation had backfired, enraging not only liberals but centrists, driving women and younger voters to the polls in record numbers. Yes, Republicans had been "able to narrowly seat Judge Kavanaugh," the *Times* reported, but in doing so they had energized "many Democrats and a share of independents in suburban congressional districts and big-state governor's races where female voters were already enraged" (*NYT* 9/29/18). On November 6, Democrats took back control of the house, winning more new seats than they had in any election since the party's 1974 post-Watergate landslide. Among the representatives elected were more than a record 100 women (*NYT* 9/30c/18: A1b, *NYT* 11/26/18).

The societalization of sexual harassment in the workplace would not be blocked by polarization. #MeToo had become deeply imbedded in American collective consciousness.

## Return to Steady State?

At the time of this writing, November 2018, the effervescence that has marked societalization – the "#MeToo moment" – has not yet subsided. Communicative media continue to publicly call out male harassers, and institutions continue to force these powerful men to resign. In the wake of "Kavanaugh," a handful of men who had been stigmatized as predators and ejected from their positions of power made efforts to return to the mainstream, presuming that there should be a return to normalcy, indeed that there already had been. Each effort, however, ignited a firestorm of passionate reproof. Jian Ghomeshi, a disgraced former Canadian Broadcasting Company star whom more than 20 women had accused of assault and harassment, published "Reflections from a Hashtag" in the *New York Review of Books* (*NYRB* 2018), a barely concealed plea for pity, sympathy, and exoneration. Its appearance on NYRB, the website of the Anglophone world's most influential intellectual magazine, immediately triggered widespread revulsion. The *Review* felt compelled to open its back pages to outraged letters expressing "shock," "utter horror," and "disgust" from readers who explained how "appalled" they were at an "absolutely disgraceful" editorial decision that brought "shame to the organization" (*NYRB* 10/25/18).

> To the Editors: I, like many others, am writing to express my distaste for the recent essay you published by Jian Ghomeshi. I have never had such a strong physical reaction of disgust while engaging in a sedentary activity like reading. It's clear that Jian still thinks *he* is the victim … Good lord! It's honestly just so embarrassing that you published [it]. (Ibid., 56)

NYRB's editorial staff apologized for "our failures" (ibid., 54) and its powerful editor, Ian Buruma, appointed with great fanfare only months earlier, was forced to resign (*NYT* 9/19/18).

"Only one of my accusers reached out or responded to my heartfelt queries," complained John Hockenberry, the former National Public Radio host, in "Exile," another long and self-absorbed mea culpa, this one published in *Harper's Magazine*. Immediately controversial, the essay generated angry pushback and critical debate (The Cut 2018). On his weekly talk show *Real Time with Bill Maher*, the popular comedic commentator Bill Maher defended Al Franken, who had resigned from the US Senate amid groping allegations, questioning the credibility of his female accusers and joking: "You know when you're a politician, being touch-feely is kind of part of the job." Maher was ridiculed as out of touch (Is It Funny or Offensive? 9/10/18). The comedian Norm Macdonald told the *Hollywood Reporter*: "It used to be, 'One hundred women can't be lying' … and then it became, 'One woman can't lie' and that became 'I believe all women'. And then you're like, 'What?'" (Huffington Post 9/12/18). Macdonald's appearance on *The Tonight Show* was canceled and his career endangered (CNN 9/12/18, *Vanity Fair* 9/12/18) When Louis C. K. – "the onetime king of stand-up who admitted to sexual misconduct with multiple women" (*NYT* 10/31/18) – returned to performing one year after his #MeToo humiliation, he was confronted with protestors holding angry signs, one of which read: "When you support Louis C. K., you tell women your laughter is more important than their sexual assaults and loss of their careers" (ibid.).

On the front page of the *New York Times*' "Sunday Review," feminist author Jennifer Weiner worried that "over the past few weeks it's felt like someone fired a start pistol [and] one by one, like bad dreams, the #MeToo men have come back" (*NYT* 9/23/18). They were now being allowed to publish their own stories, and Weiner protested it wasn't right.

> Stories matter tremendously. They're how we learn about who is real and who's less consequential; whose pain is important and whose, not much; who is the hero and who is merely the hero's reward … *Do men know how to be sorry*? (Ibid., italics added)

Such efforts by "#MeToo men" to show the time was ripe for returning to steady state had the effect of demonstrating exactly the opposite. The reactions they triggered highlighted the powerful existence of a newly gendered civil sacred. Like earlier hard-fought expansions of civil solidarity, this one would have to be fiercely protected against threats to undermine it, to demonize it, or even simply to make it seem mundane. Women's truth must be respected. It was their stories, not men's, that must now be heard. Hockenbery "demands that we consider his misery and embarrassment," the *Times*' feminist columnist Michele Goldberg angrily observed, but "he never really grapples with the misery and embarrassment he caused, never thinks deeply about how he affected the lives of the women who changed jobs to escape his advances" (*NYT* 9/16/18). Goldberg freely admitted that she, too, "mourns the loss of Franken in the Senate," but she excoriated Mahler for "seem[ing] to lack empathy for the woman who is discombobulated by suddenly feeling the hand of a man she admires on her backside." If "the discussion about #MeToo and forgiveness never seems to go anywhere," Goldberg suggested, this is "because men aren't proposing paths for restitution [but] asking why women won't give them absolution." It's not men but the gendered expansion of civil solidarity that is being betrayed.

Sooner or later, there will be a return to steady state. The question is when, and what it will mean. It seems highly doubtful that steady state will mean returning to what existed before #MeToo seized the day. Societalization produced, not just effervescence, but a new culture structure. And even after charisma has become routinized into steady state, it will leave behind not only deep cultural change, but transformed organization. The boundaries separating civil and non-civil spheres have changed; the civil–anti-civil binary is now applied to sexual behavior in the workplace in strikingly more democratic ways. There are new protagonists and antagonists, a new narrative about a female hero, a survivor telling her truth, and an expanded vision of civil solidarity inside the workplace.

Short of some "Thermidor" that brings into being a "Handmaid's Tale" dystopia, sexual harassment will join such other master signifiers of social evil as racism, anti-Semitism, and homophobia, things that cannot be said or done without powerful profanation. Which does not mean, of course, that the behaviors themselves have ceased. They continue to exist. So will sexual harassment in the workplace after societalization subsides. As long as men continue to hold asymmetrical power, there will be not only the motive, but also the means and opportunity to take advantage of female subordinates in a sexual way. When they do, however, men will now face the likelihood, or at least the very real possibility, of sanction, of being humiliated and punished. After societalization subsides, revelations of sexual harassment will still trigger moral revulsion and organizational and legal action – just not on the front page.

# Conclusion

## Societalization in Theory

The strains and crises that are the subject of this book have generated a vast social science literature, the bulk of which presents causal explanations in the realist mode. Social reactions to social problems are conceptualized as responses to objective, actually existing strains. The argument is that institutional strains create social responses, unmediated by what I have described in the preceding pages as the relatively independent culture and institutions of the civil sphere. Another way of putting this is that the focus of social scientific theories of crisis has been almost entirely intrainstitutional. "The collective definition of social problems occurs not in some vague location such as society or public opinion," Hilgartner and Bosk (1988: 58) insisted; rather it occurs in "arenas," and "if a problem arises in one institution it is likely to spread to others" (ibid., 67).

The social problem is institutional, the reaction is real, and the causal logic moves from strain to societal reaction. Is there a social crisis about media? It's because there have been "practices" of "journalistic deception" (Lasora and Dai 2007: 190). Has the "credibility of news" become an issue? It's because there has been "journalistic delinquency"

(Dickinson 2010: 2; see also Fenton 2012). A British scholar explains that the phone hacking crisis was triggered by the decline of "transparency and accountability," the result of journalism having been corporatized (Fenton 2012: 3); another lays blame on the newly deteriorating boundary between "fact and fiction" (Emmot 2011: 26–9). Investigations into financial crises have argued similarly (e.g. Berberoglu 2011, MacKenzie 2011, McCloud and Dwyer 2011, Moosvi 2010, Treas 2010, Williams 2008). An *Annual Review of Sociology* article on the 1980s savings and loan crisis found the independent variable to be the shift from industrial to postindustrial economic organization (Calavita, Tillman, and Pontell 1997); a piece in *Qualitative Sociology* recounted the "ideational foundations of financial markets and the economic events they occasion" (Ailon 2012: 252). Likewise, in the social science inquiries into the church's pedophilia crisis, social scientists laid blame on the "medieval, monarchical model of the Church" (Wilkes 2002: 105), "clerical celibacy" (O'Conaill 1995), rigid bureaucracy (Barth 2010: 780–1), insulated elites (Doyle 2006: 194), and the rollback of Vatican II reforms (Carroll 2002: 115).[1]

My complaint about this kind of social science literature concerns not its documentation of institutional strain, but the inverse relation posited between such strain and steady state – the more of the former, the less of the latter. Arguing "scandal represents a breach of institutional trust," Fine asserts that scandal "must be situated within an institutional structure" (Fine 1997: 297–8). My contention is the opposite. Steady states do not give way from institutional strains but from collective representation leveraged from the institutional outside. Social science must attenuate the putative relationship between strain and response. It is not strains that generate social crises, but societalization, a process triggered by cultural logic and media representation.

It was something like this recognition of the independent role of media representation that generated the sociology of scandal that emerged in recent decades. Gamson (2001: 197) acknowledges that sex scandals are less about sex than about "hypocrisy, recklessness, and amorality," and Thompson (1997: 39) allows that there are "transgressions of certain values, norms, and codes." Rather than conceptualizing the independent moral power of such cultural codes, however, scandal sociology instrumentalizes media representation. Thompson (1997) links indignant expressions of scandalized morality to struggles for social capital and field position, echoing Bourdieu's (1998) claim that journalism cares simply about its own "ontological glorification." Gamson (2001: 198) argues that scandals are produced because they "solve problems" for serious journalism, allowing them to compete with tabloids by transforming soft into hard news. Examining press reports on financial scandal, Williams (2008: 488) describes "media accounts" as merely "modes within a broader discourse of financial markets." Writing about the televised hearings that mark contemporary scandals, Cavender, Gray, and Miller (2010: 253) dismiss them as "theatrical spectacle[s] [that] legitimate Congress and the economic system." Adut claims that scandal-creating publicity is simply a response to "costs on third parties," explaining that "the anticipation of ... externalities is *of course* the main motivation for strategically creating scandals in the first place" (Adut 2005: 231, italics added). Describing scandals as "an episodic process of strategic interaction in public" (ibid.), Adut (2004: 532) suggests they are motivated by opportunities for "status enhancement," when "political actors ... face favorable incentives and opportunities." Because "those who take part in them are at least apparently self-interested," he explains (Adut 2012: 241), "scandals rarely entail civic or civil debate," but instead "contaminate public life with sordid stuff," serving only to "discredit institutions" (ibid.).

The roots of the reductionism that characterizes scandal sociology range from the materialism of Marx, Bourdieu, and Weber to the "situationalism" of pragmatism (Norton 2014b). The former is hardly surprising; after all, what Mann conceptualizes (approvingly) as "organizational materialism" (Mann 1993: 52) is what scandal sociology is all about. That pragmatism is the other source of instrumental, mechanistic reduction is more puzzling, for it was precisely from symbolic interactionism that an anti-realist approach to the sociology of social problems first emerged. Becker argued more than half a century ago that "deviance is not a quality of the act the person commits, but rather a consequence of the application by others of rules and sanctions" (Becker 1963: 9). In Blumer's later manifesto, he insisted, "social problems are fundamentally products of collective definition instead of existing independently as a set of objective social arrangements" (Blumer 1971: 298). Spector and Kitsuse (1977) introduced the notion of "constructing social problems" soon after, an approach that "emphasizes meaning over facts" (Harris and Best 2013: 293).

With its insistence on perception, subjectivity, and malleability, the constructionist approach to social problems bears a family resemblance to the model of societalization I have developed here. It is anticipation, however, not adumbration (Merton 1968), for the two approaches dramatically differ. What short-circuited the constructionist line? To simplify a complex story, its micro-focus was to blame: its reluctance to recognize cultural structures as social facts; its resistance to speaking the language of social spheres, institutional elites, and social power; its polemic against the very idea of society (e.g. Fine 1996). As such limitations came to be widely recognized, the search for meso- and macro-approaches led pragmatism to material rather than to cultural structures, to a narrow focus on the politics of the definitional process, and to "structural analysis" (Adut 2008: 23; cf. Fine 1997: 299) *tout court*.

The moral panics model, a theoretical high point in pragmatism's self-critical response to interactionism, dismisses the heightened moral anxiety that characterizes scandal as "ideological exploitation," describes symbolization as "exaggeration and distortion," defines social drama as "social control" and "status degradation," and dismisses journalistic outrage as "manufactured news" (Cohen 1972: 141, 43, 106, 44). Such reactions to the limits of interactional, as compared with *cultural*, pragmatics (Alexander, Giesen, and Mast 2006) throw the baby out with the bathwater. Avoiding the cultural turn, they drove into the cul-de-sac of scandal sociology. "Unmasking and debunking" (Cohen 1972: 204) may be good politics, but more is needed for it to become good sociology (see Thompson 1998: 9–10 and passim).

Theoretical resistance to the idea of societalization is not only a micro-sociological problem. Outside the late

Durkheimian tradition, macro-sociology has also had surprisingly little to say about "society" as a social fact. Modernity has been widely understood as breaking down the holism of traditional society into fragments, into economy, religion, family, law, publics, media, schools, classes, races, nations, and ethnicities – sectors that themselves have been viewed as subject to an infinite regress of fractal fragmentation. In the language of functionalism, modern social systems continuously differentiate and specialize into cooperative, reciprocating subsystems. In the language of conflict theory, functional differentiation produces warring elites, fighting classes, and the dominated and dominant fractions thereof, forming and reforming coalitions of convenience inside institutional fields.

What these otherwise divergent social theories share is the conviction that, with modernity, the whole that overarches separately organized parts has been lost. Once the morality of the social whole has given way to the logic of separate spheres, it becomes the task of social theory to explain this separation and to trace the lines of conflict and complementarity that emerge. Marx (1962 [1867]) believed that, under capitalism, the economic sphere achieved such outsized independence that it would dominate every other. Spencer (1972) thought inversely, that what characterized contemporary modernity was the differentiation of spheres and their functional complementarity. While Durkheim (1984 [1893]) believed that collective consciousness could, in principle, regulate social differentiation, in the theorizing of his middle period work he rarely specified mechanisms for doing so; in the modern conditions of his own time, he believed, intrasphere strains were unregulated and egoism and anomie held sway (Durkheim 1984 [1893]: Book III; 1966 [1897]). Weber (1958a [1946]) characterized modernity as creating conflicting and incommensurable spheres that pushed values and institutions in centrifugal directions. Parsons (Parsons and Smelser 1956) argued that cultural and material interchanges among specialized subsystems created reciprocity across institutional boundaries, insisting that cultural integration counteracted conflicts among differentiated spheres. Luhmann (1982) described social spheres as radically self-regulating, dismissing social crisis as the product of empty rhetoric. Bourdieu (1993) emphasized the growing autonomy of social fields, but related them to intrasphere struggles for vertical domination, conflating them with overarching economic divisions. Boltanski and Thévenot (2006) recognized the shifting location of institutional boundaries, but conceptualized intersphere relations as micro-negotiations among actors over sphere-specific logics.

The model of societalization advanced here challenges this widely shared macro-sociological vision of obdurate division.[2] Despite but also because of modernity, "society" remains a vigorous discursive and institutional presence. A broadly civil sphere exists that can challenge the particularistic discourses and institutional demands of separate spheres. The discourse of civil society is utopian and solidaristic, and the civil sphere's communicative and regulative institutions have the power to project this moral language beyond the boundaries of separate spheres and powerfully to reconstruct them.

These are only capacities, however, not functional inevitabilities. Spheres abut and antagonize one another; they pursue their own interests rather than aiming at some hypostasized complementarity. Perceptions of steady state camouflage strains, hiding conflicts inside the walls of institutional separation. When civil agents employ communicative and regulative resources to breach these barriers, the effect is not reciprocity but confrontation and, eventually, war between the spheres. Civil repair is possible, backlash inevitable, and standoff an unavoidable eventuality. Tensions define boundary relations, and dangerously anti-civil practices of separate spheres are sustained over long periods. Societalization does not so repair the internal functioning of spheres and their interrelations that new crises can be prevented from arising again. The fundamental divergence of institutional interests and cultures remains. During the Great Depression, Niebuhr (1934: 243), recognizing that "justice in political relations depends upon a balance of power," cautioned that "even the most imaginative political policy will fail to achieve perfect justice." In the postwar years, Aron (1950a, 1950b) similarly challenged utopian narratives about progress, describing warring elites as a permanent feature of democratic modernity. In the wake of the 1960s,

Walzer (1984) conceptualized not one sphere of justice, but many.

Social indignation flows, but it also ebbs. Yet even as societalization gives way to the illusion of steady state, the civil sphere remains restless, ready to fight another day. Societalization revives what Plato called the memory of justice. For the philosopher, justice is an ideal form that human beings are born with and that republics imitate. For the sociologist, the memory of justice is not born but made.

# Notes

## Note to Introduction

1 The empirical analyses in chapters 4–7 do not provide dispositive evidence for the societalization model but demonstrate its theoretical plausibility, which is a matter of a more preliminary nature. Can the model's key concepts be used to reconstruct a narrative of each crisis that illuminates homologous structures and phases? That mimes parallel shifts in the meanings of social actors before and after occurrences were transformed into events? That finds similar traces of elite struggles, reform opportunities, backlash efforts, and fraught, open-ended returns to the steady state? To answer these questions, I use an interpretive method – one that allows me to create a dense reconstruction of iterative empirical sequences. My aim is to hermeneutically reconstruct the shifting meanings of events and actors as they were represented in mainstream newspapers, for example *New York Times*, *Boston Globe*, *Wall Street Journal*, *USA Today*, *Financial Times*, *Guardian*, *Telegraph*, *Independent on Sunday*, and *Observer*. I examined several hundred newspaper articles produced on each topic, weighted to the 12 to 18 months after the onset of each crisis; but I also sampled longer-term developments, follow-ups, and policy outcomes. In Peircean terms, the empirical method used here is neither deductive nor inductive, but abductive (Timmermans and Tavory 2014). In the terminology of the

*Geisteswissenschaften*, the "human" (as compared with the "natural") sciences, the method is hermeneutic. Because of the positivist common sense that continues to inform so much US sociology, it is important to insist that the hermeneutical method is not a vehicle for mere description; it neither condenses information already known from other venues nor summarizes ethnographic or field observations; and is it not coding in the mechanistic understanding of computational science either (Biernacki 2012). Rather, hermeneutical reconstruction is creative, open-ended, and theory-driven (Reed 2011). It pieces together submerged, implicit, and fragmented events and speech acts into broader, more robust meaning patterns. More than abduction, this process also involves theoretical logic, as it references not only the empirical data but also pre-observational, conceptual presuppositions that underlay research programs (Lakatos 1970). What Dilthey (1976) first described as "the hermeneutical circle" – simultaneously constructing the meanings of wholes from parts and the meanings of parts from wholes – and Geertz (1973), later and rather misleadingly, dubbed "thick description" has more recently come to be called "narrative analysis" (Abbott 1992; Jacobs 1996; Sewell 1996). Because in so constructing events mass media are highly attentive to the sensibilities of those who consume their reports – the audiences of individuals who form their own understandings of contentious social processes as the latter unfold – media reports provide a privileged access to the collective consciousness. It is via competing efforts at public narration that social meanings are produced, social structures and spheres crystallized and activated, and efficient causation established. Such narrative efforts are reported on by mainstream news outlets that, at the same time, have a major role in the construction of the narratives: they not only report facts that have happened but evaluate ongoing events in terms of their own values and elite interests, thus creating new facts and new narrations. Only by tracing media representations of "events" (Mast 2006; Wagner-Pacifici 2017) can we discover the sociologically powerful (because publicly binding) interpretations that provide the evidentiary claims of this study.

# Notes to Chapter 1

1 See the table in Alexander (2006: 57–9):

| The Binary Structures of Motives | | The Binary Structures of Relationships | | The Binary Structures of Institutions | |
|---|---|---|---|---|---|
| *Civil Motives* | *Anticivil Motives* | *Civil Relationships* | *Anticivil Relationships* | *Civil Institutions* | *Anticivil Institutions* |
| Active | Passive | Open | Secretive | Rule regulated | Arbitrary |
| Autonomous | Dependent | Trusting | Suspicious | Law | Power |
| Rational | Irrational | Critical | Deferential | Equality | Hierarchy |
| Reasonable | Hysterical | Honorable | Self-interested | Inclusive | Exclusive |
| Calm | Excitable | Altruistic | Greedy | Impersonal | Personal |
| Self-controlled | Wild-passionate | Truthful | Deceitful | Contracts | Bonds of loyalty |
| Realistic | Distorted | Straightfoward | Calculating | Groups | Factions |
| Sane | Mad | Deliberative | Conspiratorial | Office | Personality |
| | | Friendly | Antagonistic | | |

2 I use the adjectives "hypothetical" and "putatively" and the verbs "appears" and "imagined" because I wish to emphasize, vis-à-vis functionalist and conflict theorizing about intersphere boundary relations, that steady state does not refer to a condition of objective equilibrium but rather to institutional insulation – a condition in which significant conflicts inside spheres are not *experienced* as threatening to the society at large. This distinction marks the difference between a mechanistic model of intersphere relations and the cultural–sociological approach I employ here. In his critique of classical economic theory, Keynes makes a similar point. While classical predictions about economic equilibrium assumed stable rates of capital investment, Keynes argues that these rates actually depend on the propensity to invest, which he equates with subjective estimations of probability. Because optimistic or pessimistic predictions about future interest rates cannot be proved objectively, Keynes argued, equilibrium depends on social conventions and collective states of mind (Keynes 1964 [1936]: 141–53).

3 Social problems that are societalized become subjects for bestselling books and award-winning movies. The financial crisis was cinematized, e.g. in *Too Big to Fail* (2011) and *The Big Short* (2015), church pedophilia, in *Doubt* (2008) and *Spotlight* (2015). Watergate was memorialized in *All the President's Men*, both the book (Woodward and Bernstein 1974) and the movie (1976), and, four decades later, two of its civil heroes, Ben Bradlee and Katherine Graham, were cinematized once again, in *The Post* (2017). The societalization of McCarthyism also continues to be memorialized, e.g. in the 2005 film *Good Night, and Good Luck*.

# Notes to Chapter 2

1 Framing theory can be helpful in thinking through the conditions that affect whether code switching succeeds and, more broadly, whether the performances of civil agents successfully fuse with the citizen audience. Drawing from Goffman's late theorizing, symbolic interactionists investigated how social movements frame their messages so as to align them with non-movement audiences. "Framing processes link individuals and groups ideologically," Hunt, Benford, and Snow (1994: 185) argued, "by placing relevant sets of actors in time and space and by attributing characteristics to them that suggest specifiable relationships." These inscriptions into time and space create protagonists, antagonists, and audiences, they explained, converting social facts into the textual resources for social performances (ibid., 186). What's missing from such perceptive formulations is a macro-account of the cultural and institutional structures within which meaning-making efforts at frame alignment are made. Systemic and institutional, such structures are not simply an "interactional accomplishment" (ibid., 190), not merely "meanings produced in the course of interactions with other individuals and objects of attention" (Snow and Benford 1988: 198).

2 Symbolic interactionist theorists concentrate on this level of agency in theorizing the construction of deviance, moral panics, and scandals; see e.g. Becker's (1963) "moral entrepreneurs," or Fine's (1997) "reputational entrepreneurs." These forms of purely pragmatic theorizing, however, often reduce agency to the cynical pursuit of self-interest. For example, when Cohen warns that "the presence alone [of] values does not guarantee successful ... social problem definition" and argues that "there must also be enterprise," he insists that "someone [who] takes the initiative" does so simply "on the basis of *interest*," instrumentally "*uses* publicity techniques to gain" support, and "must either be in a position of power himself or must have access to [it]" (Cohen 1972: 112, italics added).

# Notes to Chapter 3

1 Snow and Benford (1988: 205) have usefully conceptualized the conditions that do and do not allow resonance between social movement performances and citizens, pointing to

empirical credibility (fitting with "events in the world"), experiential commensurability (harmonizing with "the conditions of experience"), and narrative fidelity (resonating with the "cultural narratives" that are part of the "cultural heritage"). Such typifying resonances can occur, however, only after the relevant background representations have already been deposited by the kinds of processes I reference here, including social movements themselves (cf. Wright 2014).

2 Orson Welles' *Citizen Kane* (1941) – the dark retelling of the career of media baron and yellow journalist William Randolph Hearst – has continually been ranked high on the "best films of all time" lists. The film *To Kill a Mockingbird* (1962), based on Harper Lee's 1960 novel, starred Gregory Peck as Atticus Finch, a crusading hero against racial bigotry in a small southern town. In 2003, the American Film Institute named Finch the greatest film hero of the twentieth century.

## Note to Chapter 4

1 Despite the return to steady state in the United States, American newspapers have continued to conduct periodic investigations about institutional practices outside the country, sometimes triggering code switching and civil repair, sometimes noting how these societalizing processes have unfolded elsewhere. For example, in 2016, under the headline "Benedict's Brother Says He Was Unaware of Abuse," the *Times* reported, with revealing insinuation, that "the Rev. George Ratzinger, the elder brother of former Pope Benedict XVI, said in an interview ... that he had no knowledge that young boys in an internationally known German church choir he directed for 30 years had suffered sexual abuse" (*NYT* 1/10/16). Three months later, reporting on "efforts to address ignored reports" of abuse in the boys' choir, the *Times* headlined "Church Confronts Abuse Scandal at a Famed German Choir" (*NYT* 2/6/16). Eighteen months after that, under the headline "'Culture of Silence' Abetted Abuse of at Least 547 German Choir Boys" (*NYT* 7/18/17), the *Times* reported the findings of an "independent" investigator appointed by the Regensburg diocese where Rev. Ratzinger had once presided. The diocese had paid €450,000 to victims, the paper noted, and "the school has also moved to change its culture and instituted steps to prevent and report abuse in recent years" (*NYT* 7/18/17). The covering up of sexual abuse is exposed and condemned, but the protagonist now

doing the confronting is the church itself. Another narrative about church abuse unfolding inside the reconstituted steady state concerned an Australian cardinal. Headlining "Australian Inquiry Puts Papal Aide on Defense," the *Times* (*NYT* 3/1/16) reported on the video-link testimony of George Pell, former Australian archbishop and a close associate of Pope Francis. In the representation of this event, the *Times* employed terms that refer to office abuse – "how much the cardinal knew about a number of priests and brothers accused of pedophilia during the 30 years in which he rose through the ranks of Australia's clerical hierarchy," and why he had "failed to act" (*NYT* 3/1/16). These veiled accusations were sandwiched, however, between references to the effects of civil reconstruction – one outside, the other inside the church. The latter noted that Cardinal Pell was one of nine cardinals whom the reformist Francis, denouncing "the sin of covering up and denial" (*NYT* 7/7/16), had appointed to "a commission to deal with sexual abuse of children by the clergy" (*NYT* 3/1/16). The former acknowledged that Cardinal Pell had testified to the Australian Royal Commission into Institutional Responses to Child Sexual Abuse, established three years earlier. The *Times*' next installment, 16 months later, reported Cardinal Pell's arrest on sexual assault charges by Victoria, Australia police (*NYT* 6/29/17). The subsequent report communicated the news that, even as the cardinal, via a spokesman, declared himself "completely innocent," he had returned to face trial in Sydney, where he would "vigorously defend himself and clear his name" (*NYT* 7/7/17). Just hours after the cardinal's arrival in Sydney, the Royal Commission had released a cache of documents containing emails and letters relating to the abuse allegations. The *Times* quoted a former Australian abuse victim: "The first part of justice is to have the past recognized. I think the royal commission has well and truly done that" (ibid.). The last item in the story noted the declaration by Sydney's archbishop that the church would not pay for Cardinal Pell's defense (ibid.). That same day, in the editorial on its Opinion page, the *Times* headlined "The Vatican's Failure in the Abuse Scandal" (ibid.).

## Notes to Chapter 5

1 Even in foreign policy, the US government increasingly insisted that the "market knew best" and, rather than positively intervening to allay economic crises abroad, offered a "tough love"

policy that would allow the global market to solve problems and maintain a steady state (*USA Today* 9/19/08). This market first policy came to be known as the Washington Consensus, promoting deregulation and privatization as "the only path for countries seeking long-term prosperity" (ibid.).

2 My argument here is not that material consequences are inconsequential – not any more than the preceding discussion suggested that pedophilia was not, in itself, a physical violation that created psychological injury. What the model of societalization stipulates, rather, is that the nature and pathways of public discussion of the financial crisis were determined not by economic imperatives in themselves, but by the discourse and institutions of the civil sphere, as they framed the perception of economic events and of their repercussions. Max Weber allowed that "not ideas, but material and ideal interests, directly govern men's conduct"; but, he also insisted, "yet very frequently the 'world images' that have been created by 'ideas' have, like switchmen, determined the tracks along which action has been pushed by the dynamic of interest" (Weber 1958b [1946]: 280). The discourse of civil society – ideas – creates the image of the civil sphere and lays down the tracks along which the societalization of social crisis proceeds. The semiotic code switch that triggers societalization functions like a switchman on these tracks, pushing institutional elites to define and contest their material and ideal interests in distinctive ways.

3 The dangers of such moral risk are the implicit point of the German economist Hans-Werner Sinn's Cassandra-like warnings quoted in the Introduction here (see pp. 1–2). For other backlash statements of this kind, see CNBC Rick Santelli's controversial remarks that rewarding "losers" would involve the government in "promoting bad behavior" (Paeth 2012: 400 – and see below) and the apologetics of such economists as Reinhart (2011) and Kirkland (2007).

## Notes to Chapter 6

1 In its coverage of phone hacking's first criminal conviction – of a Scotland Yard official – the *Guardian* noted the significant role of the *New York Times* in prompting the new police investigation: "The offence took place as the Metropolitan police were forced to re-examine allegations of phone hacking at the *News of the World* after revelations in the *Guardian* and the *New York Times* that the activity was widespread and not just

relegated to 'one rogue reporter' as News International ... had maintained for years" (*Guardian* 1/13/13).

2 Within the broad temporal sequencing of societalization, the relationship between particular regulative and communicative interventions is path-dependent, contingent, and interactive. The renewal of Scotland Yard's investigation in the wake of the *New York Times*' story, for example, triggered both regulatory and media interventions in the United Kingdom. Even when, for nationally specific reasons, a regulative institution takes the lead position in publicly attacking anti-civil corruption (Olave 2018), the societalization of the problem depends on the code-shifting performances of communicative media.

3 Ironically, this accusation was later determined to have been inaccurate.

4 These remarks were transmitted to the press by participants in the meetings and were widely publicized.

5 Many of these cases were tried and resulted in convictions. Brooks was eventually acquitted; Colson served seven months in jail.

6 In the throes of societalization, Murdoch had split his company, News Corporation, into separate entertainment and journalistic enterprises, renaming the latter News UK.

## Notes to Chapter 7

1 In 1979, the radical feminist legal theorist Catharine A. MacKinnon wrote: "Sexual assault as experienced during sexual harassment seems less like an ordinary act of sexual desire directed toward the wrong person than an expression of dominance laced with personal contempt, the habit of getting what one wants, and the perception (usually accurate) that the situation can be safely exploited in this way – all expressed sexually. It is dominance eroticized" (MacKinnon 1979: 162). This pioneering work by MacKinnon – *Sexual Harassment of Working Women: A Case Study of Sex Discrimination* – opened the pathway toward what eventually became the legal thicket of sexual harassment law.

2 "The term 'sexual harassment' itself grew out of a consciousness-raising session Lin Farley held in 1974 as part of a Cornell University course on women and work" (Siegel 2003: 8).

3 "A Pew survey conducted in November and December 2017 found that 69 percent of Republican women thought recent allegations of harassment and assault reflected widespread

problems in society, compared with 74 percent of Democratic women" (Vox 5/7/18).

4 These data concerning the Harvey Weinstein scandal come from a search of the ProQuest database on October 5, 2017. The following headings and quotations are ordered alphabetically, by news source:

1 "El magnate Harvey Weinstein, acusado de acoso sexual toma licencia." AFP International Text Wire in Spanish.
2 "Magnata Harvey Weinstein se desculpa após alegações de assédio sexual." AFP International Text Wire in Portuguese.
3 "Film mogul Weinstein takes leave amid harassment allegations." Bloomberg Wire Service.
4 "Allegations of sexual harassment against major Hollywood producer," National Audio. Canadian Press.
5 "Harvey Weinstein apologizes." CTV National News.
6 "Harvey Weinstein takes leave from studio after harassment allegations." Dow Jones Institutional News.
7 "*New York Times* destapa historial de sepuesto acoso sexual de Harvey Weinstein: HOLLYWOOD ABUSOS." EFE News Service, Miami.
8 "Harvey Weinstein apologizes for sexual harassment." Finance Wire.
9 "Harvey Weinstein to take leave amid sexual harassment report." *Financial Times.*
10 "Daily briefing." FT.com; London.
11 "Trafficked premiere has Elizabeth Rohm but not Judd." Inner City Press; Bronx.
12 "Harvey Weinstein apologizes for sexual harassment." International Wire.
13 "Harvey Weinstein's Hollywood future is in question after sexual harassment allegations." *Los Angeles Times* (online).
14 "Harvey Weinstein unloads Connecticut home for $1.65 million." *Los Angeles Times* (online).
15 "Lena Dunham, Rose McGowan add voices to Harvey Weinstein scandal." *Los Angeles Times* (online).
16 "Harvey Weinstein to take a leave of absence amid sexual harassment claims, threatens lawsuit over report." *Los Angeles Times* (online).
17 "Hollywood exec Harvey Weinstein to take leave following sexual harassment report." The National – CBC Television; Toronto.
18 "Las Vegas, Harvey Weinstein, Spain: Your Thursday Evening Briefing." *New York Times* (Online).

19 "Actresses respond to Harvey Weinstein's accusers: 'I believe you'." *New York Times* (online).
20 "Mediaite: Turns out Harvey Weinstein is backing his feminist attorney Lisa Bloom's new show too." *Newstex Trade & Industry Blogs.*
21 "Mediaite: BOMBSHELL: NYT report accuses film mogul Harvey Weinstein of being serial sex predator." *Newstex Trade & Industry Blogs.*
22 "Mediaite: TBT: Harvey Weinstein once wrote an op-ed defending child rapist Roman Polanski." *Newstex Trade & Industry Blogs.*
23 "Mediaite: Film mogul Harvey Weinstein reportedly lawyers up ahead of explosive stories about his behavior." *Newstex Trade & Industry Blogs.*
24 "Mediaite: Democratic senators are reportedly giving Harvey Weinstein's campaign donations to charity." *Newstex Trade & Industry Blogs.*
25 "Mediaite: What exactly does *NY Times* mean by saying Harvey Weinstein 'initiated' a massage 'himself.'" *Newstex Trade & Industry Blogs.*
26 "Second opinion." PE HUB.
27 "Canadian Press budget for Thursday, October 5, 2017." Canadian Press; Montreal.
28 "Harvey Weinstein to take leave of absence after NYT exposé." *Screen International*; London.
29 "Amid harassment reports, Harvey Weinstein takes leave of absence." The Two-Way [BLOG], Washington: NPR.
30 "Harvey Weinstein takes leave from studio after harassment allegations; media report details several instances of sexual harassment by producer; Weinstein says he will 'deal with this head on.'" *Wall Street Journal* (online).
31 "Harvey Weinstein is accused of sexual harassment in explosive story, takes leave of absence." *Washington Post – Blogs* (online).
32 "Report women accuse Harvey Weinstein of sexual harassment." *Washington Post – Blogs* (online).
33 "Harvey Weinstein and Democrats' deals with Hollywood's devils: Harvey Weinstein is reminder that Hollywood's relationship with liberalism is mired in contradiction and failures of ideals." *Washington Post – Blogs* (online).

One may assume that ProQuest was unable to pick up all media reports featuring the October 5 *New York Times* story. This selection does not reflect, for example, US television and radio coverage of the story. What this list does demonstrate is the immediate uptake of the story, translation on international markets, and elaborations. Elaborations represent strategies designed to extend the original reporting so as not to make the pickup redundant – e.g. finding "fresh" angles. Such angles include editorials expounding on the hypocrisy of liberalism; Democrats placing immediate distance between Weinstein and themselves by giving his campaign donations to charity; actresses and actors showing immediate approval and support for the accusations.

5 These are *Boston Globe*, *Chicago Tribune*, *Hartford Courant*, *TCA Regional News*, *USA Today*, *Dow Jones Institutional News*, *Gulf News*, *Inner City Press*, *Los Angeles Times*, *National Post*, *New Statesman*, *New York Times*, *Newsweek*, *Philadelphia Tribune*, *Economic Times*, *Economist*, *Village Voice*, *Washington Post*, *Toronto Star*, *Variety*, *Wall Street Journal*, and *Washington Post*.

6 In the midst of this social media effervescence, it was discovered that "MeToo" had actually been introduced as a hashtag a decade earlier by Tarana Burke, an African American activist, as a means of making more visible the sexual exploitation of women of color.

7 These graphs were created by Crimson Hexagon/George Washington University.

8 This is not to suggest that other national newspapers are not also influential. Such newspapers as the *Washington Post* and the *Wall Street Journal* also break stories that drive the news cycle, as – less often – do such important regional papers as the *Boston Globe* and the *Los Angeles Times*.

9 In this reconstruction, I am not myself making the argument that newly appointed women would actually make institutional power more civil, but rather that these were the arguments made by communicative institutions as they simultaneously represented and crystallized public opinion. My point is that, in the context of societalization, men were *constructed* as anti-civil, women increasingly as civil.

10 Here is a rough survey of the most notable accusations made between October 5, 2017, and May 23, 2018, listed chronologically, by presence or absence of apology; the occupation is recorded, too:

APOLOGY:

1 Oct. 5: Harvey Weinstein – filmmaker, co-founder of Miramax

2 Oct. 10: Ben Affleck – actor, filmmaker
3 Oct. 17: Chris Savino – Nickelodeon producer
4 Oct. 19: Lockhart Steele – editorial director, Vox Media
5 Oct. 21: John Besh – celebrity chef, chief executive of Besh Restaurant Group
6 Oct. 24: Leon Wieseltier – New Republic editor
7 Oct. 25: Knight Landesman – *Artforum* publisher
8 Oct. 26: Ken Baker – E! News correspondent
9 Oct 26: Mark Halperin – MSNBC political analyst, co-author of *Game Change*
10 Oct. 29: Kevin Spacey – actor
11 Oct. 30: Hamilton Fish – New Republic president and publisher
12 Oct. 31: Michael Oreskes – NPR chief editor
13 Nov. 1: Dustin Hoffman – actor
14 Nov. 1: Jeff Hoover – Kentucky House speaker
15 Nov. 16: Al Franken – US senator (D-Minn.)
16 Nov. 20: Charlie Rose – PBS and CBS host
17 Nov. 20: Glenn Thrush – *New York Times* White House reporter
18 Nov. 21: John Lasseter – animation chief at Pixar and Disney
19 Nov. 29: Matt Lauer – host in NBC's *Today* (morning show)
20 Dec. 1: Ruben Kihuen – US House of Representatives (D-Nev.)
21 Dec. 11: Mario Batali – TV star and renowned chef
22 Dec. 13: Morgan Spurlock – Hollywood director
23 Dec. 18: Alex Kozinski – California federal court judge
24 Jan. 2: Dan Harmon – creator of *Community* and *Rick and Morty*
25 Jan. 5: Ben Vereen – Tony Award-winning actor
26 Jan. 11: James Franco – actor
27 Feb. 21: Daniel Handler – author known as Lemony Snicket
28 March 5: Sherman Alexie – Native American author
29 March 29: John Kricfalusi – creator of *The Ren & Stimpy Show*
30 May 4: Junot Diaz – author, MIT creative writing professor

NO APOLOGY:
1 Oct. 12: Roy Price – Amazon executive
2 Oct. 22: James Toback – writer-director
3 Oct. 23: Terry Richardson – fashion photographer
4 Oct. 30: Jeremy Piven – actor
5 Oct. 31: Andy Dick – comedian

6 Nov. 1: Brett Ratner – filmmaker
7 Nov. 3: David Guillod – Primary Wave Entertainment co-CEO
8 Nov. 7: Ed Westwick – actor known for *Gossip Girl*
9 Nov. 8: Jeffrey Tambor – actor
10 Nov. 9: Louis C.K. – comedian
11 Nov. 9: Roy Moore – Alabama judge and politician, US Senate candidate (R.-Ala.)
12 Nov. 9: Matthew Weiner – creator of TV series *Mad Men*
13 Nov. 16: Gary Goddard – CEO of Goddard Group, was behind the creation of theme park attractions such as the Georgia Aquarium and the Monster Plantation ride at Six Flags Over Georgia
14 Nov. 16: Eddie Berganza – editor at the DC Comics company
15 Nov. 16: Andrew Kreisberg – executive producer of TV series *Arrow*, *Supergirl*, and *The Flash*
16 Nov. 20: John Conyers – US Senator (D-Mich.)
17 Nov. 22: Nick Carter – member of the vocal group Backstreet Boys
18 Nov. 29: Garrison Keillor – creator and former host of radio show *A Prairie Home Companion*
19 Nov. 30: Russell Simmons – entrepreneur, co-founder of Def Jam Recordings
20 Dec. 6: Warren Moon – National Football League Hall of Fame quarterback, co-founder and president of Sports 1 Marketing
21 Dec. 11: Ryan Lizza – Washington correspondent of *New Yorker* magazine
22 Dec. 11: President Donald Trump
23 Dec. 15: Gene Simmons – bassist for band KISS
24 Jan. 5: Paul Haggis – Oscar-winning director and screenwriter
25 Jan. 9: Stan Lee – former editor-in-chief, publisher, chairman of Marvel Comics
26 Jan. 13: Aziz Ansari – actor, comedian
27 Jan. 13: Mario Testino – photographer
28 Jan. 14: Bruce Weber – photographer
29 Jan. 16: Seal – singer
30 Jan. 18: Michael Douglas – actor
31 Jan. 25: David Copperfield – magician
32 Jan. 27: Scott Baio – actor
33 Feb. 1: Paul Marciano – co-founder of Guess brand
34 Feb. 2: Vincent Cirrincione – talent manager
35 Feb. 16: Patrick Demarchelier – photographer

36 Feb. 16: Greg Kadel – photographer
37 Feb. 16: Andre Passos – photographer
38 Feb. 16: Seth Sabal – photographer
39 Feb. 16: David Bellemere – photographer
40 Feb. 22: Philip Berk – former president of Hollywood Foreign Press Association
41 Feb. 28: Jeff Franklin – former showrunner of American sitcom *Fuller House*
42 April 4: Nicholas Nixon – former photographer, professor at Massachusetts College of Art and Design
43 May 7: Eric Schneiderman – New York attorney general
44 May 23: Morgan Freeman – actor

Apologies: 30 out of 74 = 40.5%
No apology: 44 out of 74 = 59.5%

## Notes to Conclusion

1 I do not analyze social science literature on #MeToo because, at the time of writing, very little has appeared.

2 Of course, such broad characterizations make invisible the equivocations, ad hoc modifications, and residual categories that always shadow general theories and trigger the revisions introduced by their most acute followers. Gramsci's (1971) ideas about cultural hegemony counteracted orthodox Marxian assertions about economic domination. Bendix's (1962) emphasis on the alternation of formal and substantive justice challenged Weber's skepticism (cf. Friedland 2009) about moral challenges to legal autonomy. Smelser's (1959, 1963) attention to strains, conflict levels, moral generalization, and social movements challenged more orthodox functionalist understandings of intersphere reciprocity and steady state. Goldberg (2013) interprets Bourdieu's later work as open to the intersphere effects of civil sphere universalism, and Gorski (2013) and Townsley (2011) separate field autonomy from economic domination in order to allow relatively independent cultural processes more play. Speaking of Weber as a conflict rather than cultural theorist is also an oversimplification. Yet even Weber's (1958 [1946]) essay "Religious Rejections of the World and Their Directions" – the oblique and fascinating outlier he attached as introduction to his collected essays in the sociology of religion – proposes a view of modernity as so fractured that its values spheres are radically incommensurable.

Whether interpreted in more materialist or cultural terms, there is little disagreement that Weber powerfully resisted the notion that "society" can exert a collective moral force in modernity. Swedberg (2005: 254) writes: "[W]hile Weber occasionally uses the term 'society' ... It plays no role in his general sociology, and it is not part of his 'Basic Sociological Terms' as outlined in Ch. 1 of *Economy and Society*." Swedberg also references Frisby and Sayer's (1986: 68) assertion that, "although one of his major works is called *Economy and Society*, it does not discuss ... 'society but rather societal tendencies of action or sociation (*Vergesellschaftung*)[,] which is contrasted with action motivated by a tendency toward solidarity,'" and Kalberg's (1985: 63) argument that "it is noteworthy that Weber uses 'society' (*Gesellschaft*) only on two occasions in *Economy and Society*, both times in quotation marks." Drawing from but simultaneously distancing himself from Toennies, Weber does introduce the term *vergesellschaftung* (Weber 1978: 21 ff.), a German active noun without any direction equivalent in English but widely translated as "association," in contrast with Weber's concept of *vergemeinschaftung*: "A social relationship will be called 'communal' (*Vergemeinschaftung*) if and so far as the orientation of social action ... is based on a subjective feeling of the parties, whether affectual or traditional, that they belong together. A social relationship will be called 'associative' (*Vergesellschaftung*) if and insofar as the orientation of social action within it rests on a rationally motivated adjustment of interests" (ibid., 40–1). Weber (1978: 41) associates *Vergesellschaftung* with more modern, less traditional forms of action, for example, "rational free market exchange, which constitutes a compromise of opposed but complementary interests" and "voluntary association based on self-interest [and] the promotion of specific ulterior interests, economic or other, of its members." It is ironic but also theoretically illustrative of my broader argument that a contemporary disciple of Niklas Luhmann, Volker Schmidt (2014: 25), actually translates *Vergesellschaftung* as "societalization," equating the latter with "systemic relations whose establishment rests on mutual interests and/or instrumental concerns in contact with communal relations that involve a sense of togetherness and belongingness." I have introduced the concept of societalization with the decidedly different aim of demonstrating the continuing relevance of belonging and solidarity in contemporary societies, suggesting that modern feelings of togetherness can take civil and universalizing rather than traditionalist and particularist forms. The meaning of Durkheim's theory has also been deeply disputed. Until the late twentieth century, Durkheim's understanding of modernity was widely considered to have been constituted by the major 1890s publications – *The Division of Labor in Society* (Durkheim 1984 [1893]), *The Rules of Sociological Method* (Durkheim 1966 [1895]), and *Suicide* (Durkheim 1966 [1897]). The first and second of these books complemented Spencer's equation of modernity with functional and institutional differentiation even while acknowledging, for example, in *Division*, Book 2, Chapter 7, that some versions of the putatively premodern, mechanical solidarity of *conscience collective* would remain. *Suicide* portrayed modernity as differentiation and egoism run amok. In recent decades, however, scholars (e.g. Alexander 1982, Smith and Alexander 2005, Fournier 2012) have contrasted this middle-period emphasis on institutional division with a "cultural turn" in Durkheim's later writing, one that culminated with his work on Aboriginal religion, *The Elementary Forms of Religious Life*, first published in 1912. The impact on twentieth century sociology of this "late Durkheimian" thinking – about symbols, rituals, solidarity, and collective effervescence – was limited. It was considered foundational for the anthropology of primitive societies, not for the sociology of modernity. By contrast, contemporary cultural sociology, building specifically upon late Durkheimian thinking, has developed a more fruitful approach to contemporary modernity, one that moves beyond either/or to conceptualize the taut relation between division, solidarity, conflict, and integration. Only with late Durkheim, in the religious writings that laid the basis for contemporary cultural sociology, do we find a perspective on modernity that recognizes the continuing pulse of the social whole. The Strong Program in cultural sociology (https://ccs.yale.edu/strong-program; Alexander and Smith 2018) connects late Durkheim to such subsequent developments as semiotics, poststructuralism, symbolic anthropology, literary theory, aesthetics, and performance studies. Formulating a sociological approach to the continuing role of symbol, code, solidarity, and narrative, such cultural sociology (see Lamont 2000, Zelizer 1985) reconceptualizes modernity, bringing its meaning-centered theory and methods to bear on the core "modernist" concerns of Weber and Marx – conflict, domination, and exclusion on the one hand, possibilities for equality and incorporation on the other. Turner's model of social drama (e.g. Turner 1982) has functioned as a key link between late Durkheimian concerns and contemporary studies of conflict and reconciliation (e.g. Wagner-Pacifici 1986, Edles 1998), and it adumbrates the societalization model presented here. It describes a sequential process from breach to crisis to redress and then to reintegration or schism. The present approach differs from Turner's model by virtue of its emphasis on contingency, cultural coding, communicative and regulative institutions, and civil solidarity in contrast to *communitas*. Viewing breach in a functional rather than cultural manner, Turner failed to problematize eventness, social drama viewed through the lens of ritual theory, as a "full phases structure" intrinsic to "the developmental cycle of all groups" (Turner 1982: 75, 78) rather than as a performative achievement. For Turner, crisis is a *phase* in the unfolding of a naturalistic sequence. From the cultural–pragmatic perspective of performance theory, by contrast, crisis is a contingent outcome of cultural–institutional struggle. Because Turner's social–dramatic theory of crisis fails to recognize the growing defusion of the elements of social performance (Alexander 2011), it cannot conceptualize social crisis as a contingent, variable, culturally and institutionally conditioned response to strain.

# References

## Primary Sources

### Church Pedophilia

*Belfast Telegraph*. December 21, 2010. "Pope's child porn 'normal' claim sparks outrage among victims." http://www.belfasttelegraph.co.uk/news/world-news/popersquos-child-porn-normal-claim-sparks-outrage-among-victims-15035449.html.

*Boston Globe*. January 6, 2002. "Church allowed abuse by priest for years." https://www.bostonglobe.com/news/special-reports/2002/01/06/church-allowed-abuse-priest-for-years/cSHfGkTIrAT25qKGvBuDNM/story.html.

*Boston Globe*. January 7, 2002. "Amy Welborn's blog." http://www.amywelborn.org/2002/01/must-read-article-from-boston-globe.html.

*Boston Globe*. January 17, 2002. "AG wants church to report past abuse," Pfeiffer, Sacha and Kevin Cullen.

*Boston Globe*. January 31, 2002. "Scores of priests involved in sex abuse cases." https://www.bostonglobe.com/news/special-reports/2002/01/31/scores-priests-involved-sex-abuse-cases/kmRm7JtqBdEZ8UF0ucR16L/story.html.

*Boston Globe*. March 14, 2002. "Ex-Mass. bishop accused of ignoring abuse in NYC." Rezendes, Michael.

*Boston Globe*. May 12, 2002. "Scandal erodes traditional deference to church." Cullen, Kevin. https://www.boston

globe.com/news/special-reports/2002/05/12/scandal-erodes-traditional-deference-church/mPLNp1BFouhbpWJu9zjYxL/story.html.

*Boston Globe*. November 23, 2002. "Church tries to block public access to files." Rezendes, Michael and Walter V. Robinson. https://www.bostonglobe.com/news/special-reports/2002/11/23/church-tries-block-public-access-files/WG9WXHzF2WQuN6tCT4fy7L/story.html.

*Boston Globe*. December 1, 2002, p. A26. "Battle over files intensifies, law firm seeks court inquiry on compliance." Michael Rezendes.

*Boston Globe*. December 4, 2002. "More clergy abuse, secrecy cases." https://www.bostonglobe.com/news/special-reports/2002/12/04/more-clergy-abuse-secrecy-cases/O5QkXOZG73XodD0X5hcPzJ/story.html.

Lawlor, Philip E. 2002. "Editorial: Attitudes that must die." Bishop Accountability.org. https://www.bishop-accountability.org/resources/resource-files/media/attitude-pf.htm.

National Public Radio. January 11, 2007. "The aftermath: The church responds." Martin, Rachel. https://www.npr.org/series/6819690/scandal-in-the-church-five-years-on.

*New York Times*. March 28, 2002, p. A26. "For the faithful, trying to reconcile morality and scandal." Cohen, Patricia.

*New York Times*. April 20, 2002, p. A1. "For 2 decades, in 3 countries, priest left a trail of sex abuse." Murphy, Dean E. and Juan Forero.

*New York Times*. June 14, 2002, p. A1. "Abuse victims lay blame at feet of Catholic bishops." Goodstein, Laurie.

*New York Times*. April 3, 2010, p. WK 11. "Devil of a scandal." Dowd, Maureen.

*New York Times*. April 30, 2010, p. A4. "In abuse crisis, a church is pitted against society and itself." Donadio, Rachel.

*New York Times*. July 2, 2010, p. A1. "Amid sexual abuse, an office that failed to act." Goodstein, Laurie and David M. Halbfinger.

*New York Times*. August 15, 2011, p. A12. "Bishop in Missouri waited months to report priest, stirring parishioners' rage." Goodstein, Laurie.

*New York Times*. June 16, 2015, p. A4. "Vatican sets trial in July for ex-envoy to Caribbean." Goodstein, Laurie.

*New York Times*. January 10, 2016. "Pope Benedict's brother says he was unaware of abuse." Eddy, Melissa. https://www.nytimes.com/2016/01/11/world/europe/pope-benedicts-brother-says-he-was-unaware-of-abuse.html.

*New York Times*. February 6, 2016. "Church confronts abuse scandal at a famed German choir." Eddy, Melissa. https://www.

nytimes.com/2016/02/07/world/europe/church-confronts-abuse-scandal-at-a-famed-german-choir.html.

*New York Times*. March 1, 2016, p. A6. "Australian Inquiry Puts Papal Aide on Defensive." Elizabeth Povoledo.

*New York Times*. June 29, 2017, p. A7. "Cardinal, an Adviser to the Pope, Faces Charges of Sexual Assault in Australia." Jacqueline Williams.

*New York Times*. July 7, 2017. "The Vatican's failure in the abuse scandal." https://www.nytimes.com/2017/07/07/opinion/pope-francis-catholic-church-sexual-abuse.html.

*New York Times*. July 11, 2017, p. A5. "Cardinal George Pell returns to Australia, charged with sexual offenses." Baidawi, Adam.

*New York Times*. July 18, 2017. "'Culture of silence' abetted abuse of at least 547 German choir boys, inquiry finds." Eddy, Melissa. https://www.nytimes.com/2017/07/18/world/europe/germany-sexual-abuse-boys-choir.html.

*New York Times*. July 26, 2017. "Defrocked priest is about to be freed amid renewed fury." Seelye, Katherine Q. https://www.nytimes.com/2017/07/26/us/boston-priest-paul-shanley-sex-abuse.html.

*New York Times*. January 18, 2018, p. A4. "Sexual abuse scandal casts a pall on the pope's visit to Peru." Rochabrun, Marcelo and Andrea Zarate.

*New York Times*. January 20, 2018a, p. A10. "Pope leaves a furor in Chile, and later defends the indigenous in Peru." Rochabrun, Marcelo and Pascale Bonnefoy.

*New York Times*. January 20, 2018b, p. A22. "The pope causes priests' victims more pain." Editorial.

*New York Times*. January 23, 2018, p. A4. "Pope apologizes to abuse victims, but then again doubts claims." Horowitz, Jason.

*USA Today*. April 22, 2002a, p. 1D. "What's ahead for the church." Grossman, Cathy Lynn.

*USA Today*. April 22, 2002b, p. 6D. "Now is the time to talk." Grossman, Cathy Lynn.

*USA Today*. April 24, 2002, p. 9D. "Pope's comments draw mixed reviews." Grossman, Cathy Lynn.

*USA Today*. January 8, 2004, p. 5D. "Religious orders to conduct own audit." Grossman, Cathy Lynn.

*USA Today*. November 18, 2004, p. 4A. "Catholic bishops have had 'very tough time' new US leader says." Grossman, Cathy Lynn.

*USA Today*. February 21, 2005, p. 4D. "Studies assess the costs of clergy sex abuse scandal." Grossman, Cathy Lynn.

*Wall Street Journal*. January 18, 2002, p. W13. "Houses of worship: Abuse on trial." Molineaux, Charles.

*Wall Street Journal*. March 18, 2002, p. A18. "Unfruitful works of darkness." Bennett, William J.

*Wall Street Journal*. April 18, 2002, p. A13. "The church needs to be strong, but modern and responsive." Hunt, Albert R.

*Wall Street Journal*. April 26, 2002, p. A10. "The church and its critics."

*Wall Street Journal*. June 13, 2002, p. A4. "Americans distrust institutions in poll: Low marks go to corporate executives, brokers, drug and oil companies, the Catholic Church." Harwood, John.

## Financial Crisis

American Enterprise Institute. December 27, 2011. "Why the left is losing the argument over the financial crisis." Wallison, Peter and Edward Pinto. http://www.aei.org/publication/why-the-left-is-losing-the-argument-over-the-financial-crisis.

Competitive Enterprise Institute. June 21, 2012. "Dodd–Frank unconstitutional power-grab, says new lawsuit." Hall, Christine. https://cei.org/content/dodd-frank-unconstitutional-power-grab-says-new-lawsuit.

*Financial Times*. January 30, 2009, p. 6. "Obama attacks 'shameful' Wall Street." Guerrera, Frances and Andrew Ward.

*Financial Times*. December 24, 2009, p. 7. "Master of risk who did god's work for Goldman Sachs but won it little love." Gapper, John.

*New York Magazine*. May 22, 2010. "Obama is from Mars, Wall Street is from Venus." Heilemann, John. http://nymag.com/news/politics/66188.

*New York Times*. September 15, 2008a, p. A1. "Bids to halt financial crisis reshape landscape of Wall Street." Sorkin, Andrew Ross.

*New York Times*. September 15, 2008b, p. A1. "Financial crisis reshapes Wall Street's landscape; Merrill is sold; failing to find buyer, Lehman Bros. is set to wind down." Anderson, Jenny, Andrew Ross Sorkin, and Ben White.

*New York Times*. September 18, 2008. "Bush emerges after days of financial crisis." Goldberg, Sheryl Gay.

*New York Times*. September 19, 2008, p. A1. "Political memo: Dazed capital feels its way, eyes on the election." Calmes, Jackie.

*New York Times*. October 6, 2008. "Lehmann managers portrayed as irresponsible." Becker, Bernie and Ben White http://www.nytimes.com/2008/10/07/business/economy/07lehman.html.

*New York Times*. October 23, 2008. "Greenspan concedes error on regulation." Andrews, Edmund L. http://www.nytimes.com/2008/10/24/business/economy/24panel.html.

*New York Times*. December 2, 2008a. "Officials warn that economy will remain weak." Grynbaum, Michael M. and David Stout. http://www.nytimes.com/2008/12/02/business/economy/02bernanke.html?pagewanted=print&_r=0.

*New York Times*. December 2, 2008b, p. A1. "Recession began last December, economists say." Andrews, Edmund L.

*New York Times*. December 16, 2008, p. D5. "A crisis of confidence for masters of the universe." Friedman, Richard A.

*New York Times*. January 22, 2009. Magazine, p. 9. "The age of neo-remorse." Kirn, Walter.

*New York Times*. February 20, 2009. "Rick Santelli: Tea Party Time." Etheridge, Eric. https://opinionator.blogs.nytimes.com/2009/02/20/rick-santelli-tea-party-time.

*New York Times*. June 17, 2009. "Banks brace for fight over an agency meant to bolster consumer protection." Martin, Andrew and Louise Story.

*New York Times*. June 20, 2009. "Obama pushes financial regulatory overhaul." Cooper, Helen. http://www.nytimes.com/2009/06/21/us/politics/21radio.html.

*New York Times*. July 14, 2010. "After crisis, show of power from JPMorgan." Dash, Eric. http://www.nytimes.com/2010/07/15/business/15chase.html.

*New York Times*. July 27, 2010. "Former regulators find a home with a powerful firm." https://dealbook.nytimes.com/2010/07/27/ex-financial-regulators-get-set-to-lobby-agencies.

*New York Times*. August 5, 2010. "Wall Street faces specter of lost trading units." Bowley, Graham and Rich Dash. http://www.nytimes.com/2010/08/06/business/06wall.html.

*New York Times*. October 23, 2010. "What happened to change we can believe in?" Rich, Frank. www.nytimes.com/2010/10/24/opinion/24rich.html.

*New York Times*. November 19, 2010. "Dear S.E.C., please make brokers accountable to customers." Siegel Bernard, Tara. http://www.nytimes.com/2010/11/20/your-money/20money.html.

*New York Times*. May 1, 2011. "Springtime for bankers." Krugman, Paul. www.nytimes.com/2011/05/02/opinion/02krugman.html.

*New York Times*. July 20, 2011. "Barney Frank, financial overhaul's defender in chief." Protess, Ben. https://dealbook.nytimes.com/2011/07/20/barney-frank-financial-overhauls-defender-in-chief.

*New York Times*. February 3, 2012. "S.E.C. is avoiding tough sanctions for large banks." Wyatt, Edward.

*New York Times*. February 13, 2012. "At Volcker rule deadline, a strong pushback from Wall St." Protess, Ben and Peter Eavis. https://dealbook.nytimes.com/2012/02/13/at-volcker-rule-deadline-a-strong-pushback-from-wall-st.

*New York Times*. June 13, 2012, p. A27. "Why Berlin is balking on a bailout." Sinn, Hans-Werner.

*New York Times*. June 14, 2012, p. A1. "Church Battles Efforts to Ease Sex Abuse Suits." Laurie Goodstein and Erik Eckholm.

*New York Times*. June 15, 2012. "Rajat Gupta convicted of insider trading." Lattman, Peter and Azam Ahmed. http://dealbook.nytimes.com/2012/06/15/rajat-gupta-convicted-of-insider-trading.

*New York Times*. December 11, 2012. "Wall Street is bracing for the Dodd–Frank rules to kick in." Protess, Ben. https://dealbook.nytimes.com/2012/12/11/wall-street-is-bracing-for-the-dodd-frank-rules-to-kick-in.

*New York Times*. December 31, 2012. "Looking ahead to civil and criminal cases to come." Henning, Peter J. http://dealbook.nytimes.com/2012/12/31/looking-ahead-to-civil-and-criminal-cases-to-come.

*New York Times*. April 9, 2013a. "Former regulators find a home with a powerful firm." Protess, Ben and Jessica Silver-Greenberg. https://dealbook.nytimes.com/2013/04/09/for-former-regulators-a-home-on-wall-street.

*New York Times*. April 9, 2013b. "Not enough reform on derivatives." Editorial. www.nytimes.com/2013/04/10/opinion/not-enough-reform-on-derivatives.html.

*New York Times*. July 20, 2013. "Trying to pierce a Wall Street fog." Morgenstern, Gretchen. http://www.nytimes.com/2013/07/21/business/trying-to-pierce-a-wall-street-fog.html.

*New York Times*. September 17, 2013. 'Since Lehman's collapse, companies more forthcoming on compliance." Henning, Peter J. https://dealbook.nytimes.com/2013/09/16/since-lehmans-collapse-companies-more-forthcoming-on-compliance.

*New York Times*. April 17, 2014. "Your Thursday briefing." Hassan, Adeel and Victoria Shannon. https://www.nytimes.com/2014/04/17/us/your-thursday-briefing.html.

*New York Times*. March 20, 2015. "Despite top lawyer's fears, regulators can be held in check." Indiviglio, Daniel and Antony Currie. https://www.nytimes.com/2015/03/21/business/dealbook/despite-fears-regulators-can-be-held-in-check.html.

*New York Times*. October 5, 2017. "Randal Quarles confirmed as Federal Reserve Governor." Appelbaum, Binyamin. https://www.nytimes.com/2017/10/05/us/politics/randal-quarles-confirmed-as-federal-reserve-governor.html.

*New Yorker*. May 16, 2016, p. 38. "The financial page: Banking's new normal." Surowiecki, James.

*Rolling Stone*. July 9, 2009: "The great American bubble machine." Taibbi, Matt. http://www.rollingstone.com/politics/news/the-great-american-bubble-machine-20100405.

*USA Today*. September 19, 2008, p. 1B. "US bends the rules of free markets; nation isn't practicing what it preached to other countries." Lynch, David J.

*USA Today*. September 24, 2008, p. 11A. "Main Street's blind faith; it's the public that feeds the Wall Street Beast. In fact, now is the time to end this cyclical con game." Fishman, Ted C.

*USA Today*. October 1, 2008, p. 1B. "Wall Street's stock has dropped in world's eyes; it has ruined its reputation, so where do we go from here?" Shell, Adam.

*USA Today*. February 25, 2009, p. 1A. "'We will recover'; Everyone will have to sacrifice 'worthy priorities,' Obama says." Hall, Mimi and David Jackson.

*USA Today*. June 11, 2009, p. 1B. "Obama plan limits bonuses, golden parachutes." Gogoi, Pallavi.

*USA Today*. September 15, 2009, p. 10A. "A year after Lehman's fall, financial regulation stalls."

*USA Today*. December 14, 2009, p. 7A. "Obama: 'Fat-cat' bankers owe help to US taxpayers." Jackson, David.

*Wall Street Journal*. September 19, 2008, p. A1. "Wall Street's ills seep into everyday lives." Levitz, Jennifer, Ilan Brat, and Nicholas Casey.

*Wall Street Journal*. September 20, 2008, p. A1. "As times turn tough, New York's wealthy economize—plastic surgeons, yacht builders brace for leaner times; saying no to caviar." Gamerman, Ellen, Cheryl Lu-Lien Tan, and Francine Schwadel.

*Wall Street Journal*. September 24, 2008, p. A1. "Rescue plan stirs calls for deeper regulation." Scannell, Kara, Phred Dvorak, Joann S. Lublin, and Elizabeth Williamson.

*Wall Street Journal*. October 10, 2008, p. A1. "As banking 'fairy tale' ends, Iceland looks back to the sea." Forelle, Charles.

*Wall Street Journal*. October 24, 2008, p. A1. "Greenspan admits errors to hostile panel." Scannell, Kara and Sudeep Reddy.

*Wall Street Journal*. February 25, 2009, p. A1. "Obama seeks to snap gloom: President says economy will emerge stronger: Push on health, energy, education." Weisman, Jonathan.

YouTube. February 19, 2009. "Rick Santelli and 'The Rant of the Year.'" https://www.youtube.com/watch?v=bEZB4taSEoA.

## Phone Hacking

*Adweek*. June 20, 2011. "The devil's due: Will the guardian bring down Rupert Murdoch?" Wolff, Michael. http://www.adweek.com/michael-wolff/devils-due-132653.

*Congressional Record: Proceedings and Debates of the 106th Congress*. First Session, Volume 145, Part. 14, August 4, 1999 to August 5, 1999. Washington, United States Printing Office.

*Guardian*. February 3, 2007. "Memo to all editors: Do not tap this man's phone." Robinson, James. http://www.guardian.co.uk/media/2007/feb/04/pressandpublishing.business?INTCMP=SRCH.

*Guardian*. July 9, 2009. "News of the World phone hacking: Muddying the water avoids the real question." Davies, Nick. http://www.guardian.co.uk/media/2009/jul/09/phone-hacking-analysis-nick-davies.

*Guardian*. July 4, 2011. "Missing Molly Dowler's voicemail was hacked by News of the World." Davies, Nick and Amelia Hill. http://www.guardian.co.uk/uk/2011/jul/04/milly-dowler-voicemail-hacked-news-of-world.

*Guardian*. July 5, 2011. "Families of 7/7 victims 'were targets of phone hacking.'" Robinson, James, Amelia Hill, Sam Jones, Nick Davies, and Dan Sabbagh. http://www.guardian.co.uk/media/2011/jul/06/families-7–7-targets-phone-hacking?INTCMP=SRCH.

*Guardian*. July 6, 2011. "News of the World investigator may have targeted families of dead soldiers." Robinson, James. http://www.guardian.co.uk/media/2011/jul/06/news-world-investigator-families-dead-soldiers?INTCMP=SRCH.

*Guardian*. July 8, 2011a. "News of the World closure: What the papers say." Greenslade, Roy. https://www.theguardian.com/media/greenslade/2011/jul/08/national-newspapers-newsoftheworld.

*Guardian*. July 8, 2011b. "Phone hacking and sacrilege." Lynch, Gordon. http://www.guardian.co.uk/commentisfree/belief/2011/jul/08/phone-hacking-and-sacrilege/print.

*Guardian*. July 9, 2011. "Last day at the News of the World: Sombre, surreal and defiant." Beaumont, Peter and Cherry Wilson. http://www.guardian.co.uk/media/2011/jul/09/last-day-news-of-the-world?INTCMP=SRCH.

*Guardian*. July 13, 2011. "Murdoch media dynasty descends from deal to disaster." Martinson, Jane and Patrick Wintour. http://www.guardian.co.uk/media/2011/jul/13/murdoch-media-dynasty-deal-disaster?INTCMP=SRCH.

*Guardian*. July 24, 2011. "Lord Justice Leveson." http://www.guardian.co.uk/media/2011/jul/24/lord-justice-leveson-mediaguardian-100–2011?INTCMP=SRCH.

*Guardian*. November 2, 2011. "Leveson inquiry: Yes, let's be honest, we do have two presses." Greenslade, Roy. http://www.guardian.co.uk/media/greenslade/2011/nov/28/leveson-inquiry-hughgrant?INTCMP=SRCH.

*Guardian*. December 15, 2011. "Milly Dowler hacking was tip of the iceberg." Sabbagh, Dan. http://www.guardian.co.uk/media/2011/dec/15/milly-dowler-hacking-news-of-the-world?INTCMP=SRCH.

*Guardian*. April 25, 2012. "Rupert Murdoch: I sacked Harold Evans to head off *Times* rebellion." https://www.theguardian.com/media/2012/apr/25/rupert-murdoch-harold-evans-times.

*Guardian*. April 26, 2012a. "Rupert Murdoch admits NoW phone hacking culture of cover-up." Sabbagh, Dan. https://www.theguardian.com/media/2012/apr/26/murdoch-admits-phone-hacking-coverup.

*Guardian*. April 26, 2012b. "Rupert Murdoch predicts newspapers could die out in 10 years." https://www.theguardian.com/media/2012/apr/26/rupert-murdoch-predicts-newspapers-may-die.

*Guardian*. June 12, 2012. "Leveson inquiry: Ed Miliband, Harriet Harman, Sir John Major Appear." Holliday, Josh and Dugald Baird. http://www.guardian.co.uk/media/2012/jun/12/leveson-inquiry-miliband-harman-major-live?INTCMP=SRCH.

*Guardian*. January 13, 2013. "Police officer found guilty of trying to sell information to News of the World." Laville, Sandra. http://www.guardian.co.uk/uk/2013/jan/10/police-guilty-trying-sell-information?INTCMP=SRCH.

*Guardian*. October 10, 2013. "Press regulation: Leveson distances himself from Royal Charter." O'Carroll, Lisa and Josh Halliday. https://www.theguardian.com/media/2013/oct/10/press-regulation-leveson-recommendations-lost.

*Guardian*. April 13, 2015. "Labour vows to protect media plurality and implement Leveson proposals." Jasper Jackson. https://www.theguardian.com/media/2015/apr/13/labour-media-plurality-leveson-manifesto-ed-miliband.

*Guardian*. April 27, 2015. "Operation Elveden: Police and CPS Face Criticism after Not Guilty Verdicts." Press Association. https://www.theguardian.com/uk-news/2015/apr/27/operation-elveden-police-cps-criticism-not-guilty-journalists.

*Guardian*. April 21, 2016. "John Whittingdale 'not minded' to implement Leveson in full." Martinson, Jane. https://www.theguardian.com/media/2016/apr/21/john-whittingdale-leveson-press-regulation-costs-implement.

*Guardian*. November 1, 2016. "Leveson: Bradley raises doubts about press–police relations inquiry." Martinson, Jane. https://www.theguardian.com/media/2016/nov/01/leveson-bradley-questions-value-of-press-police-relations-inquiry.

*Guardian*. December 22, 2016. "Karen Bradley appears to play down need for new press regulation." Sparrow, Andrew.

https://www.theguardian.com/media/2016/dec/22/karen-bradley-appears-play-down-need-new-press-regulation.

Leveson Report. 2012. *An Inquiry into the Culture, Practices, and Ethics of the Press*, 4 vols. https://www.gov.uk/government/uploads/system/uploads/attachment_data/file/270939/0780_i.pdf.

Media Policy Project Blog. January 8, 2014. "It's 2014 and we're still implementing Leveson recommendations." London School of Economics. http://blogs.lse.ac.uk/mediapolicyproject/2014/01/08/its-2014-and-were-still-implementing-leveson-inquiry-recommendations.

*New York Times*. March 16, 1989, p. A31. "At home abroad: *News of the World*." Lewis, Anthony.

*New York Times*. September 5, 2010. Magazine, p. 30. "Hack attack!" Van Natta, Don, Jo Becker, and Graham Bowley.

*New York Times. July* 6, 2011. "Murdoch facing parliament's ire in hacking case." Sarah Lyall. http://www.nytimes.com/2011/07/07/world/europe/07britain.html?pagewanted=all.

*New York Times*. July 21, 2011, p. A11. "In court, suggestions of hacking beyond the *News of the World*." Becker, Jo and Ravi Somaiya.

*New York Times*. May 1, 2012. "Panel in hacking case finds Murdoch unfit as news titan." Burns, John F. and Ravi Somaiya.

*New York Times*. July 24, 2014. "Ex-tabloid executive acquitted in British phone hacking case." Bennhold, Katrin and Alan Cowell. https://www.nytimes.com/2014/06/25/world/europe/rebekah-brooks-found-not-guilty-in-phone-hacking-case.html.

*New York Times*. November 29, 2015. "Murdoch's British tabloids clean up their acts." Lyall, Sarah. https://www.nytimes.com/2015/11/30/business/media/murdochs-british-tabloids-clean-up-their-acts.html.

*New York Times*. November 30, 2015, p. B1. "Getting the scoop on the up and up." Lyall, Sarah.

*New Yorker*. April 2, 2012, pp. 50–9. "Mail supremacy: The newspaper that rules Britain." Collins, Lauren. http://www.newyorker.com/reporting/2012/04/02/120402fa_fact_collins.

*Telegraph*. July 4, 2011. "Milly Dowler's phone was hacked by the 'News of the World.'" http://www.telegraph.co.uk/news/uknews/crime/8616409/Milly-Dowlers-phone-was-hacked-by-News-of-The-World.html.

*Telegraph*. July 7, 2011. "Phone hacking: Families of war dead 'targeted' by *News of the World*." Hughes, Mark, Duncan Gardham, John Binghman, and Andy Bloxham. http://www.telegraph.co.uk/news/uknews/phone-hacking/8621797/Phone-hacking-families-of-war-dead-targeted-by-News-of-the-World.html.

*USA Today*. July 8, 2011, p. 2B. "Murdoch shutters 'News of the World.'"
*USA Today*. July 20, 2011, p. 1B. "Murdoch has his 'most humble day.'" Stauss, Gary and Traci Watson.
*USA Today*. July 22, 2011, p. 8A. "After decades of buccaneering, Murdoch runs up against limits."
*USA Today*. July 26, 2011, p. 9A. "How good could come from Murdoch's 'low journalism'." Wickham, DeWayne.
*Wall Street Journal*. July 13, 2011, p. A15. "Law & order, Fleet Street." Jenkins, Jr., Holman W.
*Wall Street Journal*. July 14, 2011, p. A1. "News Corp. caves as support fades." Cimilluca, Dana and Alistair McDonald.
*Wall Street Journal*. July 20, 2011, p. A1. "Murdochs are grilled." Bryan-Low, Cassell and Paul Sonne.
*Wall Street Journal*. July 25, 2012, p. B1. "Hacking charges filed: Eight people, including two former top UK tabloid editors, accused of conspiring." Sonne, Paul and Jeanne Whalen.
*Wall Street Journal*. November 21, 2012, p. B4. "Corporate news: UK bribe probe leads to charges." Whalen, Jeanne and Paul Sonne.
Ward, Philip. March 4, 2014. "The Leveson Report: Implementation." House of Commons Library. http://researchbriefings.parliament.uk/ResearchBriefing/Summary/SN06535#fullreport.
WBUR. 2014. "British phone-hacking scandal brought to a close." http://hereandnow.wbur.org/2014/06/24/phone-hacking-verdict.

## #MeToo

*The American Conservative*. April 19, 2018. "Six months in, #MeToo has become infantilizing and authoritarian." Williams, Joanna.
*Atlanta Journal Constitution*. March 16, 2018. "#MeToo slow in coming – and kept mostly out of view – at Georgia Capitol." Getz, J. https://politics.myajc.com/news/state--regional-govt--politics/metoo-slow-coming-and-kept-mostly-out-view-georgia-capitol/WpH2h8JbREv02Ev3JjAQaM.
Barron's. April 24, 2018. "When your team members mock #MeToo." Ragatz, Julie.
BillTrack50. February 15, 2018. "#MeToo, Time's up and the legislation behind the movement." Evelynn, Sarah.
*Bloomberg Businessweek*. December 20, 2017. "How to make better men: The #MeToo movement is slowly eliciting change in cultural institutions that help define masculinity." Suddath, Claire.
Breitbart News. September 19, 2018. "Haven Monahan to testify at

Kavanaugh hearings." Coulter, Ann. https://www.breitbart.com/politics/2018/09/19/ann-coulter-haven-monahan-to-testify-at-kavanaugh-hearings.

Breitbart News. February 14, 2018. "Cassie Jaye on #MeToo: 'Falsely accused people are victims, too.'" Kraychick, Robert.

Challenger, Gray & Christmas. 2018. Press release: "#MeToo survey update: more than half of companies reviewed sexual harassment policies." https://www.challengergray.com/press/press-releases/metoo-survey-update-more-half-companies-reviewed-sexual-harassment-policies.

*Chicago Sun Times*. March 21, 2018. "Until celebrities said 'me too,' nobody listened to blue-collar women about assault." Altmayer, Karla.

CNBC. May 31, 2018. "In the wake of #MeToo, companies turn to private investigators to identify predators in their ranks." Picker, Leslie and Harriet Taylor. https://www.cnbc.com/2018/05/31/companies-are-turning-to-private-investigators-to-identify-harassers.html.

CNN. September 12, 2018. "Norm Macdonald apologizes after #MeToo comments." France, Lisa Respers. https://www.cnn.com/2018/09/12/entertainment/norm-macdonald-metoo-apology/index.html.

*Colorado Springs Independent*. November 8, 2017a, p. 13. "The profound prevalence." Simison, C. https://www.csindy.com/coloradosprings/the-profound-prevalence-of-the-metoo-movement/Content?oid=8467727

*Colorado Springs Independent*. November 8, 2017b. "#WhoHasn't." Eurich, Laura. https://www.csindy.com/coloradosprings/whohasnt/Content?oid=8467730

The Cut. September 12, 2018. "Hockenberry accusers speak out after *Harper*'s publishes essay." Ryan, Lisa. https://www.thecut.com/2018/09/john-hockenberry-accusers-harpers-essay.html.

Dallas News. October 16, 2017. "#MeToo brings Dallas stories of sexual assault to social media." Jaramillo, Cassandra, Brendan Meyer, and Nancy Churnin. https://www.dallasnews.com/life/digital-life/2017/10/16/metoo-brings-dallas-stories-sexual-harassment-assault-social-media.

*Digiday*. February 5, 2018. "Agencies rethink their dating policies in the #MeToo era." Lffreing, Ilyse. https://digiday.com/marketing/agencies-rethink-dating-policies-metoo-era.

*Forbes*. September 17, 2018. "#MeToo after Moonves: What should companies be doing?" Levick, Richard.

Fortune. December 19, 2017. "Microsoft changes its sexual harassment policies in the wake." Morris, Chris.

Fortune. July 18, 2018. "Employers are clamping down on the office romance in the #MeToo era." Zillman, Claire.

Glennbeck.com. August 15, 2018. "#MeToo is coming after its own." https://www.glennbeck.com/glenn-beck/metoo-is-coming-after-its-own.

*Guardian*. December 1, 2017. "Alyssa Milano on the #MeToo movement: 'We're not going to stand for it any more.'" Sayej, Nadja. https://www.theguardian.com/culture/2017/dec/01/alyssa-milano-mee-too-sexual-harassment-abuse.

*Guardian*. September 18, 2018. "McDonald's workers walk out in 10 US cities over 'sexual harassment epidemic.'" Anonymous. https://www.theguardian.com/business/2018/sep/18/mcdonalds-walkout-workers-protest-sexual-harassment-epidemic.'

Hannity Fox News. January 8, 2018. "Exposing Hollywood hypocrisy amid Oprah 2020 rumors." https://video.foxnews.com/v/5705538885001/?#sp=show-clips.

*Hartford Courant*. October 22, 2017. "#All of Us: Why #MeToo is taking off." Tolland, L. M.

*Hollywood Reporter*. May 3, 2018. "Roman Polanski, Bill Cosby booted from Film Academy." Konerman, Jennifer and Gregg Kiladay. https://www.hollywoodreporter.com/news/roman-polanski-bill-cosby-booted-academy-1108390.

Huffington Post. April 7, 2011. "Sex scandals in science." Brooks, Michael. https://www.huffingtonpost.co.uk/michael-brooks/sex-scandals-of-science_b_889755.html?guccounter=1&guce_referrer_us=aHR0cHM6Ly93d3cuZ29vZ2xlLmNvbS8&guce_referrer_cs=8IXl18mKVypsWZLoiYR8FA.

Huffington Post. September 12, 2018. "Norm Macdonald thinks Me Too will lead to a celebrity 'sticking a gun in his head'." Wanshel, Elyse. https://www.huffingtonpost.com/entry/norm-macdonald-me-too-movement_us_5b97fceee4b0511db3e6b3de.

Is It Funny or Offensive? September 10, 2018. "Bill Maher takes heat for Indians joke, dismissing Michelle Goldberg in Al Franken segment." https://isitfunnyoroffensive.com/bill-maher-takes-heat-for-indians-joke-dismissing-michelle-goldberg-in-al-franken-segment.

*Jacksonville Free Press*. December 7, 2017. "#Churchtoo: Women share stories of sexual abuse involving the church." Anonymous.

KHOU 11. October 17, 2017. "Houston women join #MeToo Movement." Bludau, J. https://www.khou.com/article/news/local/houston-women-join-metoo-movement/484065817.

*Los Angeles Times*. October 7, 2017. "The problem of sexual harassment is much bigger than Hollywood's vile 'casting couch' culture." Los Angeles Times Editorial Board. http://www.latimes.

com/opinion/editorials/la-ed-weinstein-harassment-20171007-story.html.

*Los Angeles Times*. October 11, 2017, p. A12. "Enabling Harvey Weinstein." Los Angeles Times Editorial Board.

*Los Angeles Times*. September 17, 2018. "A generation after Clarence Thomas, the Senate heads for another battle over judging allegations of sexual misconduct." Lauter, David. http://www.latimes.com/politics/la-na-pol-kavanaugh-debate-20180917-story.html.

Market Watch. July 14, 2018. "In the wake of #MeToo, more US companies reviewed their sexual harassment policies." Buchwald, E.

Market Watch. February 16, 2018. "What shareholders should know about their investments and #MeToo." Lamagna, M.

*Miami Times*. November 19, 2017, p. 2A. "#MeToo: A hashtag for change." Anonymous.

*Monterey County Weekly*. October 26, 2017. "Speaking up." Dunn, M.

NBC News. October 7, 2016. "Trump on hot mic: 'When you're a star ... you can do anything' to women." Timm, Jane C. https://www.nbcnews.com/politics/2016-election/trump-hot-mic-when-you-re-star-you-can-do-n662116.

National Conference of State Legislatures. June 6, 2018. "2018 legislation on sexual harassment in the legislature." http://www.ncsl.org/research/about-state-legislatures/2018-legislative-sexual-harassment-legislation.aspx.

National Public Radio. October 3, 2018. "Poll: More believe Ford than Kavanaugh: A cultural shift from 1991." Montanaro, Domenico.

*New Jersey Jewish News*. October 19, 2017. "Weinstein scandal's 'Big Bang' in Orthodox community." Dreyfus, Hannah.

*New York Review of Books*. October 11, 2018. "Reflections on a Hashtag." Ghomeshi, Jian.

*New York Review of Books*. October 25, 2018, pp. 54–58. "Responses to 'Reflections on a Hashtag.'" O., Joanne, et al. https://www.nybooks.com/articles/2018/10/25/responses-to-reflections-from-a-hashtag.

*New York Times*. April 1, 2017. "Bill O'Reilly thrives at Fox News, even as harassment settlements add up." Steel, Emily and Michael S. Schmidt. https://www.nytimes.com/by/emily-steel.

*New York Times*. October 5, 2017. "Harvey Weinstein paid off sexual harassment accusers for decades." Kantor, Jodi and Megan Twohey. https://www.nytimes.com/2017/10/05/us/harvey-weinstein-harassment-allegations.html.

*New York Times*. October 7, 2017. "The pigs of liberalism."

Douthat, Ross. https://www.nytimes.com/2017/10/07/opinion/sunday/harvey-weinstein-harassment-liberals.html.

*New York Times*. October 10, 2017. "Gretchen Carlson: How to encourage more women to report sexual harassment." Carlson, Gretchen. https://www.nytimes.com/2017/10/10/opinion/women-reporting-sexual-harassment.html.

*New York Times*. October 15, 2017. "How to break a sexual harassment story." Symonds, A.

*New York Times*. October 17, 2017, p. A23. "The myth of the progressive prosecutor." Rice, J.D.

*New York Times*. October 23, 2017. "After Weinstein scandal, a plan to protect models." Friedman, V. https://www.nytimes.com/2017/10/23/fashion/sexual-harassment-law-models-new-york-state-harvey-weinstein.html.

*New York Times*. November 5, 2017, p. A25. "A conspiracy of inaction on sexual abuse." Leonhardt, David.

*New York Times*. December 14, 2017. "The politics of him too." Edsell, Thomas B. https://www.nytimes.com/2017/12/14/opinion/democratic-party-sexual-misconduct.html.

*New York Times*. January 9, 2018. "Catherine Deneuve and others denounce the #MeToo movement." Safronova, Valeriya. https://www.nytimes.com/2018/01/09/movies/catherine-deneuve-and-others-denounce-the-metoo-movement.html.

*New York Times*. March 23, 2018. "#MeToo called for an overhaul: Are workplaces really changing?" Kantor, J.

*New York Times*. March 24, 2018, p. A1. "#MeToo inspires, but change won't come easy." Kantor, J.

*New York Times*. April 4, 2018. "#MeToo has done what the law could not." MacKinnon, Catharine A. https://www.nytimes.com/2018/02/04/opinion/metoo-law-legal-system.html.

*New York Times*. April 16, 2018. "*New York Times* and *New Yorker* share Pulitzer for Public Service." Grynbaum, Michael M. https://www.nytimes.com/by/michael-m-grynbaum.

*New York Times*. June 28, 2018. "After #MeToo, the ripple effect." Bennett, Jessica.

*New York Times*. September 13, 2018a, p. B1. "Another executive's head rolls at besieged CBS." Koblin, John and Michael M. Brynbaum.

*New York Times*. September 13, 2018b, p. A1. "Revelation of Moonves's deceit was last straw for CBS board." Stewart, James.

*New York Times*. September 16, 2018, p. SR9. "The shame of the MeToo men." Goldberg, Michelle.

*New York Times*. September 18, 2018, p. B1. "Delivering a message to McDonald's." Abrams, R.

*New York Times*. September 19, 2018. "*New York Review of Books* editor is out amid uproar over #MeToo Essay." Buckley, Cara.

*New York Times*. September 23, 2018, p. SR1. "The patriarchy will always have its revenge." Weiner, Jennifer.

*New York Times*. September 27, 2018. "On politics with Lisa Lerer: He litigated, she persuaded." Lerer, Lisa. https://www.nytimes.com/2018/09/27/us/politics/on-politics-kavanaugh-blasey-ford-testimony.html.

*New York Times*. September 29, 2018. "Kavanaugh could help GOP in Senate midterms, but not in house races." Martin, Jonathan and Alexander Burns. https://www.nytimes.com/2018/09/29/us/politics/kavanaugh-republicans-midterms.html.

*New York Times*. September 30a, 2018, p. A23. "Court pick steals a page from Trump's playbook on white male anger." Peters, Jeremy W. and Susan Chira.

*New York Times*. September 30b, 2018, p. A1a. "Fight over Kavanaugh shows the power, and limits, of #MeToo." Zernike, K. and Emily Steel.

*New York Times*. September 30c, 2018, p. A1b. "For nominee, GOP takes a big gamble." Martin, Jonathan and Alexander Burns.

*New York Times*. September 30d, 2018, p. SR8. "What America owes women." Gay, Mara.

*New York Times*. October 23, 2018. "#MeToo brought down 201 powerful men: Nearly half of their replacements are women." Carlsen, Audrey et al.

*New York Times*. October 24, 2018. "In 'A star is born,' equality is deadly." Dargis, Manohla.

*New York Times*. October 31, 2018, p. C1. "Louis C. K. performs, and it's no secret." Deb, Sopan.

*New York Times*. November 7, 2018, p. A29. "'It was all fake,' Trump says in Kavanaugh ploy." Baker, Peter.

*New York Times*. November 9, 2018. "Facebook to stop forced arbitration cases." Wakabayashi, Daisuke and Jessica Silver-Greenberg. https://www.nytimes.com/2018/11/09/technology/facebook-arbitration-harassment.html.

*New York Times*. November 26, 2018. "'Kavanaugh's revenge' fell short against Democrats in the midterms." Hulse, Carl. https://www.nytimes.com/2018/11/25/us/politics/kavanaugh-midterm-elections.html.

*New Yorker*. October 10, 2017. "From aggressive overtures to sexual assault: Harvey Weinstein's accusers tell their stories." Farrow, R.

*Newsweek*. November 17, 2017. "A senior Fox News analyst thinks a man can't be alone with a woman without sexually assaulting her." Solis, Marie. https://www.newsweek.com/senior-fox-news-analyst-thinks-man-cant-be-alone-woman-without-sexually-714920.

*Numéro*. April 12, 2018. "'All the other designers hate me…' Karl Lagerfeld gets ready to tell all." Utz, Philip. https://www.numero.com/en/fashion/interview-karl-lagerfeld-chanel-virgil-abloh-j-w-anderson-azzedine-alaia.

PEW Stateline. July 31, 2018. "#MeToo has changed our culture, now it's changing our laws." Beitsch, Rebecca. https://www.pewtrusts.org/en/research-and-analysis/blogs/stateline/2018/07/31/metoo-has-changed-our-culture-now-its-changing-our-laws.

Pillsbury Insights. October 8, 2018. "California laws change legal landscape on sexual harassment." Weber, Paula and Cara Adams. https://www.pillsburylaw.com/en/news-and-insights/california-laws-change-harassment-landscape.html.

PR News. October 23, 2017. "8 Days Later, #MeToo movement expands well beyond entertainment industry." Wood, Samantha.

*Real Estate in Depth*. September 2018. "The new NYS sexual harassment law requirements take effect on Oct. 9, 2018." Dolgetta, John. http://www.realestateindepth.com/legal-advocacy/the-new-nys-sexual-harassment-law-requirements-take-effect-on-oct-9.

RedState Blog. November 29, 2017. "NY Times Editorial Board moves from opinion journalism into straight-up political activism." Lee, Sarah.

RedState Blog. September 24, 2018. "Democrats have launched the era of #MeToo McCarthyism." Slager, Brad.

*Santa Barbara Independent*. October 26, 2017. "Schools on #MeToo track." Hamm, K.

*Time*. April 11, 2016. "A brief history of sexual harassment in America before Anita Hill." Cohen, Sascha. http://time.com/4286575/sexual-harassment-before-anita-hill.

*Time*. February 21, 2017. "Uber hires former Attorney-General Eric Holder to review sexual-harassment claims." Patnaik, Subrat.

*Time*. December 18, 2018. "The silence breakers." Zacharek, Stephanie, Eliana Dockterman and Haley Sweetland Edwards. http://time.com/time-person-of-the-year-2017-silence-breakers.

US Equal Employment Opportunity Commission. n.d. "Sexual harassment." https://www.eeoc.gov/laws/types/sexual_harassment.cfm.

*USA Today*. October 8, 2018, p. B1. "#MeToo movement may have unintended consequences." Ortiz, Jorge J.

*Vanity Fair*. September 12, 2018. "Tonight show axes norm MacDonald sit-down after controversial interview." Bradley, Laura. https://www.vanityfair.com/hollywood/2018/09/norm-macdonald-metoo-louis-ck-roseanne-barr-tonight-show-canceled.

Vox. May 7, 2018. "Republican women care about sexual harassment, but their party isn't listening." North, Anna. https://www.vox.com/2018/5/7/17272336/sexual-harassment-metoo-me-too-movement-trump-republicans-roy-moore.

*Washington Post*. August 2, 2016. "One reporter owns the Roger Ailes story: Here's why he says it's not over." Sullivan, Margaret. https://www.washingtonpost.com/lifestyle/style/one-reporter-owns-the-roger-ailes-story-heres-why-he-says-its-not-over/2016/08/02/42d49004–5832–11e6–9aee-8075993d73a2_story.html?utm_term=.b12ca5d5135d.

*Washington Post*. October 8, 2016. "Trump recorded having extremely lewd conversation about women in 2005." Fahrenthold, David A. https://www.washingtonpost.com/politics/trump-recorded-having-extremely-lewd-conversation-about-women-in-2005/2016/10/07/3b9ce776–8cb4–11e6-bf8a-3d26847eeed4_story.html?utm_term=.4cd88dcdae.

*Washington Post*. October 13, 2017. "From Quentin Tarantino to Barack Obama, big names are speaking out against Harvey Weinstein." Butler, Bethonie. https://www.washingtonpost.com/news/arts-and-entertainment/wp/2017/10/09/more-big-names-are-speaking-out-against-harvey-weinstein-heres-what-theyre-saying/?utm_term=.793702a93ad3.

*Washington Post*. October 16, 2017. "#MeToo made the scale of sexual abuse go viral: But is it asking too much of survivors?" Ohlheiser, Abby.

*Washington Post*. October 19, 2017. "The woman behind 'Me Too' knew the power of the phrase when she created it – 10 years ago." Ohlheiser. Abby.

*Washington Post*. December 7, 2017. "Al Franken's resignation: He followed in the footsteps of Sen. Bob Packwood." Phillips, Kristine. https://www.washingtonpost.com/news/retropolis/wp/2017/11/22/before-franken-and-moore-there-was-sen-bob-packwood-a-serial-sexual-harasser-reelected-anyway/?utm_term=.d1104e57c912.

*Washington Post*. January 25, 2018. "The #MeToo Movement Will Be in Vain." Lenhoff, D.

*Washington Post*. September 26, 2018. "How #MeToo has changed the DC power structure – so far." Gerhart, Ann and Danielle Rindler. https://www.washingtonpost.com/graphics/2018/politics/how-metoo-has-changed-the-dc-power-structure/?utm_term=.0e9a62345879.

*Washington Post*. October 22, 2018. "How #MeToo really was different, according to data." Ohlheiser, Abby.

Wenzel Fenton Cabassa, P.A. January 1, 2018. "A history of sexual harassment laws in the United States." Fenton, Matthew K. https://www.wenzelfenton.com/blog/2018/01/01/history-sexual-harassment-laws-united-states.

Winston & Strawn LLP. June 14, 2018. "Legislative trends: 'Me Too' movement and sexual harassment disclosure laws." Grumet-Morris, Aviva. https://www.winston.com/en/thought-leadership/legislative-trends-me-too-movement-and-sexual-harassment-disclosure-laws.html.

Workforce. April 3, 2018. "HR responds to the #MeToo movement." Rafter, Michelle V. https://www.workforce.com/2018/04/03/hr-responds-metoo-movement-2.

## Secondary Sources

Abbott, Andrew. 1992. "From causes to events: Notes on narrative positivism." *Sociological Methods and Research* 20(4): 428–55.

Adut, Ari. 2004. "Scandal as norm entrepreneurship strategy: Corruption and the French investigating magistrates." *Theory and Society* 33(5): 529–78.

Adut, Ari. 2005. "A theory of scandal: Victorians, homosexuality, and the fall of Oscar Wilde." *American Journal of Sociology* 111(1): 213–48.

Adut, Ari. 2008. *On Scandal: Moral Disturbances in Society, Politics, and Art*. New York: Cambridge University Press.

Adut, Ari. 2012. "A theory of the public sphere." *Sociological Theory* 30(4): 238–62.

Ailon, Galit. 2012. "The discursive management of financial risk scandals: The case of *Wall Street Journal* commentaries on LTCM and Enron." *Qualitative Sociology* 35(3): 251–70.

Alexander, Jeffrey C. 1981. "The mass news media in systemic, historical, and comparative perspective," pp. 17–52 in E. Katz and T. Szecsko, eds., *Mass Media and Social Change*. London: SAGE.

Alexander, Jeffrey C. 1982. *The Antinomies of Classical Thought: Marx and Durkheim*. Berkeley: University of California Press.

Alexander, Jeffrey C. 1988. "Culture and political crisis: Watergate and Durkheimian Sociology," pp. 187–224 in J. Alexander, ed., *Durkheimian Sociology: Cultural Studies*. Cambridge: Cambridge University Press.

Alexander, Jeffrey C. 2001. "The long and winding road: Civil repair of intimate injustice." *Sociological Theory* 19(3): 371–400.

Alexander, Jeffrey C. 2003. "On the social construction of moral universals: The 'holocaust' from war crime to trauma drama," pp. 27–83 in J. C. Alexander, *The Meanings of Social Life: A Cultural Sociology*. New York: Oxford University Press.

Alexander, Jeffrey C. 2006. *The Civil Sphere*. New York: Oxford University Press.

Alexander, Jeffrey C. 2010. *The Performance of Politics: Obama's Victory and the Democratic Struggle for Power*. New York: Oxford University Press.

Alexander, Jeffrey C. 2011. *Performance and Power*. Cambridge: Polity.

Alexander, Jeffrey C. 2018. "The societalization of social problems: Church pedophilia, phone hacking, and the financial crisis." *American Sociological Review* 83(6): 1049–78.

Alexander, Jeffrey C., Elizabeth Breese, and Maria Luengo, eds. 2016. *The Crisis of Journalism Reconsidered: Cultural Power*. New York: Cambridge University Press.

Alexander, Jeffrey C., Ron Eyerman, Bernhard Giesen, and Neil J. Smelser, eds. 2004. *Cultural Trauma and Collective Identity*. Berkeley and Los Angeles: University of California Press.

Alexander, Jeffrey C., Bernhard Giesen, and Jason L. Mast, eds. 2006. *Social Performance: Symbolic Action, Cultural Pragmatics, and Ritual*. Cambridge: Cambridge University Press.

Alexander, Jeffrey C. and Bernadette Jaworsky. 2014. *Obama Power.* Cambridge: Polity.

Alexander, Jeffrey C., Anna Lund, and Andrea Voyer, eds. 2019. *The Nordic Civil Sphere*. New York: Cambridge University Press.

Alexander, Jeffrey C., David Palmer, Sunwoong Park, and Agnes Shuk-mei Ku, eds. 2019. *The Civil Sphere in East Asia*. New York: Cambridge University Press.

Alexander, Jeffrey C., and Philip Smith. 2018. "The strong program in cultural sociology: Meaning first," pp. 13–22 in L. Grindstaff, J. R. Hall, and M. Lo, eds., *Routledge Handbook of Cultural Sociology*, 2nd edn. New York: Routledge.

Alexander, Jeffrey C., Trevor Stack, and Farhad Khoshrokovar, eds. 2019. *Breaching the Civil Order: Radicalism and the Civil Sphere*. New York: Cambridge University Press.

Alexander, Jeffrey C. and Carlo Tognato, eds. 2018. *The Civil Sphere in Latin America*. New York: Cambridge University Press.

Allen, Henry. 2007. "A journalist for whom there were not enough words." *Washington Post*, April 25. http://www.washingtonpost.com/wp-dyn/content/article/2007/04/24/AR2007042402512.html.

Aron, Raymond. 1950a. "Social structure and the ruling class: Part 1." *British Journal of Sociology* 1(1): 1–16.

Aron, Raymond. 1950b. "Social structure and the ruling class: Part 2." *British Journal of Sociology* 1(2): 126–43.

Austin, John. 1957. *How to Do Things with Words*. Cambridge, MA: Harvard University Press.

Barth, Tom. 2010. "Crisis management in the Catholic Church: Lessons for public administrators." *Public Administration Review* 70(5): 780–91.

Barthes, Roland. 1977. "Introduction to the structural analysis of narratives," pp. 79–124 in Roland Barthes, *Image/Music/Text*. New York: Hill and Wang.

Becker, Howard S. 1963. *Outsiders: Studies in the Sociology of Deviance*. New York: Free Press.

Beeson, Ed. 2015. "Trial ace: Keker & Van Nest's John Keker." *Law360*, August 25. https://www.law360.com/articles/694295/trial-ace-keker-van-nest-s-john-keker (available on subscription).

Bendix, Reinhard. 1962. *Max Weber: An Intellectual Portrait*. Garden City, NY: Anchor Books.

Ben-Veniste, Richard. 2009. *The Emperor's New Clothes: Exposing the Truth from Watergate to 9/11*. New York: St. Martin's.

Berberoglu, Berch. 2011. "The global capitalist crisis: Its origins, dynamics and impact on the United States." *International Review of Modern Sociology* 37(2): 159–84.

Biernacki, Richard. 2012. *Reinventing Evidence in Social Inquiry*. New York: Palgrave Macmillan.

Blumer, Herbert. 1971. "Social problems as collective behavior." *Social Problems* 18(3): 298–306.

Boltanski, Luc and Laurent Thévenot. 2006. *On Justification: Economies of Worth*, translated by Catherine Porter. Princeton, NJ: Princeton University Press.

Bourdieu, Pierre. 1993. *The Field of Cultural Production: Essays on Art and Literature*, edited and introduced by Randal Johnson. New York: Columbia University Press.

Bourdieu, Pierre. 1998. *On Television*, translated by Priscilla Parkhurst Ferguson. New York: New Press.

Bradlee, Ben. 1991. "Talking with David Frost." Channel 13. New York Public Television, September 27.

Bradlee, Ben. 1995. *A Good Life: Newspapering and Other Adventures*. New York: Simon & Schuster.

Bradlee, Ben, Jr. 2002. "Introduction," pp. ix–xiii in Investigative Staff of the *Boston Globe*, *Betrayal: The Crisis in the Catholic Church*. Boston, NJ: Little, Brown and Company.

Branch, Taylor. 1988. *Parting of the Waters: America in the King Years, 1954–63*. New York: Simon & Schuster.

Breese, Elizabeth. 2011. *Interpreting the News: A Cultural Sociology of Journalistic Discourses in the United States*. Unpublished PhD dissertation, Yale University.

Bruni, Frank and Elinor Burkett. 2002 [1993]. *A Gospel of Shame*. New York: Harper.

Bruyn, Severyn T. 2000. *A Civil Economy: Transforming the Market in the Twenty-First Century*. Ann Arbor: University of Michigan Press.

Calavita, K., R. Tillman, and H. N. Pontell. 1997. "The savings and loan debacle, financial crime, and the state." *Annual Review of Sociology* 23: 19–38.

Carroll, James. 2002. "On the crisis in Catholicism." *Daedalus* 131(3) (Special issue *On Education*): 114–16.

Cavender, Gray, Kishonna Gray, and Kenneth W. Miller. 2010. "Enron's perp walk: Status degradation ceremonies as narrative." *Crime, Media, Culture* 6: 251–66.

Chandler, Alfred D. 1977. *The Visible Hand: The Managerial Revolution in American Business*. Cambridge, MA: Harvard University Press.

Cohen, Michael. 2018. "The #MeToo movement findings from the PEORIA Project." Public Echoes of Rhetoric in America (PEORIA) Project, George Washington University. https://gspm.gwu.edu/sites/g/files/zaxdzs2286/f/downloads/2018%20RD18%20MeToo%20Presentation.pdf.

Cohen, Stanley. 1972. *Folk Devils and Moral Panics: The Creation of the Mods and Rockers*. London: MacGibbon & Kee.

Comey, James B. 2013. "Fidelity, bravery, and integrity: The essence of the FBI." Speech at installation as director, October 23. https://www.fbi.gov/news/speeches/fidelity-bravery-and-integrity-the-essence-of-the-fbi.

Cott, Nancy F. 1987. *The Grounding of Modern Feminism*. New Haven, CT: Yale University Press.

Cottle, Simon. 2004. *The Racist Murder of Steven Lawrence: Media Performance and Public Transformation*. Westport, CT: SAGE.

Cottle, Simon. 2011. "Mediatized disasters in the global age: On the ritualization of catastrophe," pp. 259–83 in J. Alexander, R. N. Jacobs, and P. Smith, eds., *The Oxford Handbook of Cultural Sociology*. New York: Oxford University Press.

Darrow, Clarence. 1961. *Attorney for the Damned: Clarence Darrow in the Courtroom*. Chicago, IL: University of Chicago Press.

Dees, Morris. 2011. *A Lawyer's Journey: The Morris Dees Story*. Chicago, IL: American Bar Association.

Dickinson, Roger D. 2010. "Making up the news: Journalists, deviance, and social control in news production," pp. 223–33 in Stuart Allan, ed., *The Routledge Companion to News and Journalism Studies*. London: Routledge.

Dilthey, Wilhelm. 1976. *Selected Writings*, edited and introduced by H. P. Rickman. New York: Cambridge University Press.

Douglas, Mary. 1966. *Purity and Danger: An Analysis of Concepts of Pollution and Taboo*. New York: Praeger.

Doyle, Thomas P. 2006. "Clericalism: Enabler of clergy sexual abuse." *Pastoral Psychology* 54(3): 189–213.

Durkheim, Émile. 1966 [1895]. *The Rules of Sociological Method*. New York: Free Press.

Durkheim, Émile. 1966 [1897]. *Suicide*. New York: Free Press.

Durkheim, Émile. 1984 [1893]. *The Division of Labor in Society*. New York: Free Press.

Dyan, Daniel and Elihu Katz. 1992. *Media Events*. Cambridge, MA: Harvard University Press.

Edles, Laura. 1998. *Symbol and Ritual in the New Spain*. New York: Cambridge University Press.

Emmot, Bill. 2011. "Unholy trinity." *RSA Journal* 157(5547): 26–9.

Eyerman, Ron. 2006. "Performing opposition or, how social movements move," pp. 193–217 in J. C. Alexander, B. Giesen, and J. L. Mast, eds., *Social Performance: Symbolic Action, Cultural Pragmatics, and Ritual*. New York: Cambridge University Press.

Eyerman, Ron, J. C. Alexander, and E. Breese, eds. 2011. *Narrating Trauma*. Boulder, CO: Paradigm Publishers.

Eyerman, Ron and Andrew Jamison. 1991. *Social Movements: A Cognitive Approach*. Cambridge: Polity.

Fenton, Natalie. 2012. "Telling tales: Press, politics, power, and the public interest." *Television and New Media* 13: 3–6.

Fine, Gary Alan. 1996. "Reputational entrepreneurs and the memory of incompetence: Melting supporters, partisan warriors, and images of President Harding." *American Journal of Sociology* 101(5): 1159–93.

Fine, Gary Alan. 1997. "Scandal, social conditions, and the creation of public attention: Fatty Arbuckle and the 'problem of Hollywood.'" *Social Problems* 44(3): 297–323.

Foner, Eric. 1988. *Reconstruction: America's Unfinished Revolution, 1863–1877*. New York: HarperCollins.

Fournier, Marcel. 2012. *Émile Durkheim: A Biography*. Cambridge: Polity.

Fraser, Nancy. 1992. "Rethinking the public sphere: A contribution to the critique of actually existing democracy," pp. 109–42 in C. Calhoun, ed., *Habermas and the Public Sphere*. Cambridge: MIT Press.

Frederickson, George M. 1971. *The Black Image in the White Mind: The Debate on Afro-American Character and Destiny, 1817–1914*. New York: Harper & Row.

Frederickson, George M. 1981. *White Supremacy: A Comparative Study in American and South African History*. New York: Oxford.

Friedland, Roger. 2009. "Institution, practice, and ontology: Toward a religious sociology," pp. 45–84 in R. Meyer, K. Sahlin-Andersson, M. Ventresca, and P. Walgenbach, eds., *Institutions and Ideology: Research in the Sociology of Organizations*, vol. 27. Bingley: Emerald Group Publishing.

Friedland, Roger and Robert R. Alford. 1991. "Bringing society back in: Symbols, practices, and institutional contradictions," pp. 232–63 in W. W. Powell and P. DiMaggio, eds., *The New Institutionalism in Organizational Analysis*. Chicago, IL: University of Chicago Press.

Friedland, Roger and A. F. Robertson, eds. 1990. *Beyond the Marketplace*. New York: Aldine de Gruyter.

Friend, Tad. 2015. "Dan and Bob." *New Yorker*. November 2. https://www.newyorker.com/magazine/2015/11/02/dan-and-bob.

Frisby, David and Derek Sayer. 1986. "The ambiguity of modernity: George Simmel and Max Weber," pp. 422–33 in Wolfgang Mommsen and Jurgen Osterhammel, eds., *Max Weber and His Contemporaries*. London: Unwin.

Gamson, Joshua. 2001. "Normal sins: Sex scandal narratives as institutional morality tales." *Social Problems* 48(2): 185–205.

Geertz, Clifford. 1973. *The Interpretation of Cultures*. New York: Basic Books.

Goldberg, Chad. 2013. "Struggle and solidarity: Civic republican elements in Boudieu's political sociology." *Theory and Society* 42(4): 369–94.

Gorski, Philip. 2013. "Conclusion: Bourdieusian theory and historical analysis: Maps, mechanisms, and methods," pp. 327–66 in P. Gorski, ed., *Bourdieu and Historical Analysis*. Durham, NC: Duke University Press.

Graham, Katherine. 1997. *Personal History*. New York: Vintage.

Gramsci, Antonio. 1971. *Selections from the* Prison Notebooks *of Antonio Gramsci*. London: Lawrence & Wishart.

Griffiths, Richard. 1991. *The Use of Abuse: The Polemics of the Dreyfus Affair and its Aftermath*. New York: Oxford University Press.

Gross, Neil. 2009. "A pragmatist theory of social mechanisms." *American Sociological Review* 74(3): 358–79.

Guthrie, Julian. 2014. "John Keker relishes the fight in the courtroom." *Chronicle*, October 13. https://www.sfgate.com/bayarea/article/John-Keker-relishes-the-fight-in-the-courtroom-3622831.php.

Hallin, Daniel C. and Paolo Mancini. 2004. *Comparing Media Systems: Three Models of Media and Politics*. New York: Cambridge University Press.

Hallock, Steven M. 2010. *Reporters Who Made History: Great American Journalists on the Issues and Crises of the Late 20th Century*. Santa Barbara, CA: ABC-Clio.

Harris, Scott R. and Joel Best. 2013. "Three questions for constructionism," pp. 285–94 in Joel Best and Scott R. Harris, eds., *Making Sense of Social Problems: New Images, New Issues*. Boulder, CO and London: Lynne Rienner.

Havill, Adrian. 1993. *Deep Truth: The Lives of Bob Woodward and Carl Bernstein*. New York: Birch Lane Press.

Henderson, Jennifer. 2016. "Ex-Greenberg Traurig litigator seeks redemption for sex abuse victims." January 8. https://www.law.com/americanlawyer/almID/1202746674729/ExGreenberg-Traurig-Litigator-Seeks-Redemption-for-Sex-Abuse-Victims/?slreturn=20180221132649.

Hilgartner, Stephen and Charles L. Bosk. 1988. "The rise and fall of social problems: A public arenas model." *American Journal of Sociology* 94(1): 53–78.

Hirschman, Albert O. 1991. *The Rhetoric of Reaction: Perversity, Futility, Jeopardy*. Cambridge, MA: Harvard University Press.

Hofstader, Richard. 1955. *The Age of Reform: From Bryan to FDR*. New York: Knopf.

House of Commons, Culture, Media and Sport Committee. 2010. *Press Standards, Privacy, and Libel: Second Report of 2009–10*, vol. 2. London: Stationery Office Ltd. https://publications.parliament.uk/pa/cm200910/cmselect/cmcumeds/362/362ii.pdf.

Hunt, Scott A., Robert D. Benford, and David A. Snow. 1994. "Identity fields: Framing processes and the social construction of movement identities," pp. 185–208 in Enrique Larana, Hank Johnston, and Joseph Gusfield, eds., *New Social Movements*. Philadelphia, PA: Temple University Press.

Investigative Staff of the *Boston Globe*. 2002. *Betrayal: The Crisis in the Catholic Church*. Boston, NJ: Little, Brown and Company.

Isely, Paul J. 1997. "Child sexual abuse and the Catholic Church: An historical and contemporary review." *Pastoral Psychology* 45(4): 277–99.

Jacobs, Ronald N. 1996. "Civil society and crisis: Culture, discourse, and the Rodney King beating." *American Journal of Sociology* 101: 1238–72.

Jacobs, Ronald N. 2000. *Race, Media, and the Crisis of Civil Society: From Watts to Rodney King*. Cambridge: Cambridge University Press.

Jenkins, Philip. 1996. *Pedophiles and Priests: Anatomy of a Contemporary Crisis*. New York: Oxford University Press.

Kalberg, Stephen. 1985. "The role of ideal interests in Max Weber's comparative historical sociology," pp. 46–67 in Robert Antonio and Ronald Glassman, eds., *A Weber–Marx Dialogue*. Lawrence: University Press of Kansas.

Kane, Anne. 2019. "The civil sphere and the Irish Republican movement, 1970–1998," n.p., in Jeffrey C. Alexander, T. Stack, and F. Khoshrokovar, eds., *Breaching the Civil Order: Radicalism and the Civil Sphere*. New York: Cambridge University Press.

Kerber, Linda K. and Jane Sherron De Hart, eds. 1995. *Women's America: Refocusing the Past*. New York: Oxford University Press.

Keynes, John Maynard. 1964 [1936]. *The General Theory of Employment, Interest, and Money*. New York: Harcourt Brace Jovanovich.

Kirkland, Rik. 2007. "Rupert Murdoch." *Foreign Policy*, 158: 24–26, 28, 30.

Kivisto, Peter and Giuseppe Sciortino, eds. 2015. *Solidarity, Justice, and Incorporation: Thinking through* The Civil Sphere. New York: Oxford University Press.

Knausgaard, Karl Ove. 2018. *The End: My Struggle, Book 6*, trans. Don Bartlett and Martin Aitken. London: Random House/Harvill Secker.

Kristeva, Julia. 1980. *Desire in Language: A Semiotic Approach to Language and Art*, edited by Leon S. Roudiez. New York: Columbia University Press.

Ku, Agnes. 1998. "Boundary politics in the public sphere: Openness, secrecy, and leak." *Sociological Theory* 16(2): 172–92.

Lakatos, Imre. 1970. "Falsification and the methodology of scientific research programs," pp. 91–196 in I. Lakatos and A. Musgrave, eds., *Criticism and the Growth of Knowledge*. Cambridge: Cambridge University Press.

Lamont, Michele. 2000. *The Dignity of Working Men*. Cambridge, MA: Harvard University Press.

Landes, Joan B. 1988. *Women and the Public Sphere in the Age of the French Revolution*. Ithaca, NY: Cornell University Press.

Lasora, Dominic L. and Jia Dai. 2007. "Newsroom's normal accident?" *Journalism Practice* 1(2): 159–74.

Lee, Hee-Jeong. 2018. "Boundary tension and reconstruction: Credit information crises and the civil sphere in Korea," pp. 60–83 in Jeffrey C. Alexander, D. Palmer, S. Park, and A. Ku, eds., *The Civil Sphere in East Asia*. New York: Cambridge University Press.

Lewis, Neil A. 2001. "Man in the news: A man made for law enforcement – Robert Swan Mueller III." *New York Times*, July 6.

Lothstein, L. M. 1993. "Can a sexually addicted priest return to ministry after treatment? Psychological issues and possible forensic solutions." *Catholic Lawyer* 34(1): 89–113.

Luengo, Maria. 2018. "Shaping civil solidarity in Argentina: The power of the civil sphere in repairing violence against women," pp. 39–65 in J. C. Alexander and C. Tognato, eds., *The Civil Sphere in Latin America*. New York: Cambridge University Press.

Luhmann, Niklas. 1982. *The Differentiation of Society*. New York: Columbia University Press.

MacKenzie, Donald. 2011. "The credit crisis as a problem in the sociology of knowledge." *American Journal of Sociology* 116(6): 1778–9 and 1841.

MacKinnon, Catherine. 1979. *Sexual Harassment of Working Women: A Case Study of Sex Discrimination*. New Haven, CT: Yale University Press.

Mann, Michael. 1993. *The Sources of Social Power*, vol. 2: *The Rise of Classes and Nation-states, 1760–1914*. Cambridge: Cambridge University Press.

Mann, Michael. 2013. *The Sources of Social Power*, vol. 4: *Globalizations, 1945–2011*. New York: Cambridge University Press.

Marrus, Michael R. and Robert O. Paxton. 1981. *Vichy France and the Jews*. Stanford, CA: Stanford University Press.

Marshall, Thomas H. 1965. *Class, Citizenship, and Social Development*. New York: Free Press.

Marx, Karl. 1962 [1867]. *Capital*, vol. 1. Moscow: International Publishers.

Massey, Douglas S. and Nancy A. Denton. 1993. *American Apartheid: Segregation and the Making of the Underclass*. Cambridge, MA: Harvard University Press.

Mast, Jason. 2006. "The cultural pragmatics of event-ness: The Clinton/Lewinsky affair," pp. 115–45 in J. Alexander, B. Giesen, and J. Mast, eds., *Social Performances: Symbolic Action, Cultural Pragmatics, and Ritual*. Cambridge: Cambridge University Press.

Mast, Jason. 2012. *The Performative Presidency: Crisis and Resurrection during the Clinton Years*. Cambridge: Cambridge University Press.

McCloud, Laura and Rachel E. Dwyer. 2011. "The fragile American: Hardship and financial troubles in the 21st century." *Sociological Quarterly* 52(1): 13–35.

Meacham, Andrew. 2011. "Pulitzer-winning former St. Petersburg Times reporter Bette Orsini dies at 85." *St.*

*Petersburg Times*, March 29. https://www.culteducation.com/group/1284-scientology/25269-pulitzer-winning-former-st-petersburg-times-reporter-bette-orsini-dies-at-85.html.

Merton, Robert K. 1968. "On the history and systematics of sociological theory," pp. 1–38 in Robert K. Merton, *Social Theory and Social Structure*. New York: Free Press.

Moosvi, Shireen. 2010. "Capitalism and crises: Toward economic change." *Social Scientist* 38(7/8): 29–43.

Morgenstern, Joe. 2015. "'Spotlight' review: Blazingly bright, fearlessly focused." *Wall Street Journal*, November 5. https://www.wsj.com/articles/spotlight-review-blazingly-bright-fearlessly-focused-1446750534.

Myers, John E. B. 2008. "A short history of child protection in America." *Family Law Quarterly* 42(3): 449–63.

National Review Board for the Protection of Children and Young People. 2004. *A Report on the Crisis in the Catholic Church in the United States*. Washington, DC: US Conference of Catholic Bishops.

Ngai, Pun and Kenneth Tsz Fung Ng. 2019. "Attempting civil repair in China: SACOM's campaigns and the challenge to digital capitalism," pp. 148–66 in J. C. Alexander, D. Palmer, S. Park, and A. Ku, eds., *The Civil Sphere in East Asia*. New York: Cambridge University Press.

Niebuhr, Reinhold. 1934. *Reflections on the End of an Era*. New York and London: Charles Scribner's Sons.

Norton, Matthew. 2014a. "Classification and coercion: The destruction of piracy in the English maritime system." *American Journal of Sociology* 119(6): 1573–5.

Norton, Matthew. 2014b. "Mechanisms and meaning structures." *Sociological Theory* 32(2): 162–87.

O'Conaill, Sean. 1995. "Scandals in the church: Challenge and opportunity." *Studies: An Irish Quarterly Review* 84(333): 21–7.

Olave, Maria Angelica Thumala. 2018. "Civil indignation in Chile: Recent collusion scandals in the retail industry," pp. 66–91 in J. C. Alexander and C. Tognato, eds., *The Civil Sphere in Latin America*. New York: Cambridge University Press.

Ostertag, Stephen. 2019. "Anti-racism movements and the US civil sphere: The case of black lives matter," in J. C. Alexander, T. Stack, and F. Khoshrokovar, eds., *Breaching the Civil Order: Radicalism and the Civil Sphere*. New York: Cambridge University Press.

Paeth, Scott R. 2012. "The great recession: Some Niebuhrian reflections." *Soundings: An Interdisciplinary Journal* 95(4): 389–410.

Parsons, Talcott and Neil J. Smelser. 1956. *Economy and Society*. New York: Free Press.

Pateman, Carole. 1988. "The fraternal social contract," pp. 101–28 in J. Keane, ed., *Civil Society and the State: New European Perspectives*. London: Verso.

Pfohl, Stephen J. 1977. "The 'discovery' of child abuse." *Social Problems* 24(3): 310–23.

Polanyi, Karl. 1944. *The Great Transformation: The Political and Economic Origins of our Time*. Boston, MA: Beacon.

Reed, Isaac. 2011. *Interpretation and social knowledge: On the Use of Theory in the Human Sciences*. Chicago, IL: University of Chicago Press.

Reed, Isaac. 2013. "Charismatic performance: A study of Bacon's rebellion." *American Journal of Cultural Sociology* 1(2): 254–87.

Reinhart, Vincent. 2011. "A year of living dangerously: The management of the financial crisis in 2008." *Journal of Economic Perspectives* 25(1): 71–90.

Revers, Matthias. 2017. *Contemporary Journalism in the US and Germany: Agents of Accountability*. New York: Palgrave Macmillan.

Roberts, Sam. 2017. "E. Clinton Bamberger, defense lawyer with a 'fire for justice,' is dead at 90." *New York Times*, February 17: B13.

Rueschemeyer, Dietrich. 1986. *Power and the Division of Labor*. Stanford, CA: Stanford University Press.

Russell, Charles Edward. 1933. *Bare Hands and Stone Walls: Some Recollections of a Sideline Reformer*. New York: Charles Scribner's Sons.

Said, Edward. 1978. *Orientalism*. New York: Random House.

Samuelsohn, Darren. 2017. "Everything we know about the Mueller probe so far." *Politico*, June 6. https://www.politico.com/story/2017/06/06/mueller-russia-probe-trump-239163.

Schmidt, Volker H. 2014. *Global Modernity: A Conceptual Sketch*. New York: Palgrave.

Schudson, Michael. 1978. *Discovering the News: A Social History of American Newspapers*. New York: Basic Books.

Schudson, Michael. 2003. *The Sociology of the News*. New York: W. W. Norton.

Scott, A. O. 2015. "Review: In 'Spotlight': The *Boston Globe* digs up the Catholic Church's dirt." *New York Times*, November 5. https://www.nytimes.com/2015/11/06/movies/review-in-spotlight-the-boston-globe-digs-up-the-catholic-churchs-dirt.html.

Seidman, Steven. 1992. *Embattled Eros: Sexual Politics and Ethics in Contemporary America*. New York: Routledge.

Sewell, William H., Jr. 1996. "Historical events as transformations of structures: Inventing revolution at the Bastille." *Theory and Society* 25: 841–81.

Shils, Edward. 1975. "Center and periphery," pp. 3–15 in Edward

Shils, *Center and Periphery and Other Essays in Macro-Sociology*. Chicago, IL: University of Chicago Press.

Siegel, Rieva B. 2003. "A short history of sexual harassment," pp. 1–39 in Catherine A. MacKinnon and Rieva B. Siegel, eds., *Directions in Sexual Harassment Law*. New Haven, CT: Yale University Press.

Smelser, Neil J. 1959. *Social Change in the Industrial Revolution: An Application of Theory to the British Cotton Industry*. Chicago, IL: University of Chicago Press.

Smelser, Neil J. 1963. *Theory of Collective Behavior*. New York: Free Press.

Smith, Philip. 1991. "Codes and conflict: Towards a theory of war as ritual." *Theory and Society* 20: 103–38.

Smith, Philip. 2005. *Why War? The Cultural Logic of Iraq, the Gulf War, and Suez*. Chicago, IL: University of Chicago Press.

Smith, Philip and Jeffrey C. Alexander. 2005. "Introduction: The new Durkheim," pp. 1–40 in J. Alexander and P. Smith, eds., *The Cambridge Companion to Durkheim*. New York: Cambridge University Press.

Smith, Philip and Nicolas Howe. 2015. *Climate Change as Social Drama: Global Warming in the Public Sphere*. New York: Cambridge University Press.

Snow, David A. and Robert D. Benford. 1988. "Ideology, frame resonance, and participant mobilization." *International Social Movements Research* 1: 197–217.

Somers, Margaret R. 2008. *Genealogies of Citizenship: Markets, Statelessness and the Right to Have Rights*. Cambridge: Cambridge University Press.

Sorkin, Andrew Ross. 2009. *Too Big to Fail: The Inside Story of How Wall Street and Washington Fought to Save the Financial System from Crisis – and Themselves*. New York: Viking Press.

Spector, Malcolm and John I. Kitsuse. 1977. *Constructing Social Problems*. Menlo Park, CA: Cummings.

Spencer, Herbert. 1972. *Herbert Spencer on Social Evolution: Selected Writings*, edited by J. D. Y. Peel. Chicago, IL: University of Chicago Press.

Starkman, Dean. 2011. "Confidence game: The limited vision of the news gurus." *Columbia Journalism Review*, November 8. http://www.cjr.org/essay/confidence_game.php.

Starkman, Dean. 2014. *The Watchdog that Didn't Bark: The Financial Crisis and the Disappearance of Investigative Journalism*. New York: Columbia University Press.

Stone, I. F. 1963. "A word about myself." Website of I. F. Stone. http://ifstone.org/biography.php.

Swedberg, Richard. 2005. *Max Weber Dictionary*. Stanford, CA: Stanford University Press.

Tavory, Iddo and Ann Swidler. 2009. "Condom semiotics: Meaning and condom use in rural Malawi." *American Sociological Review* 74: 174–89.

Thompson, John B. 1997. "Scandal and social theory," pp. 34–64 in James Lull and S. Hinerman, eds., *Media Scandals: Morality and Desire in the Popular Culture Marketplace*. New York: Columbia University Press.

Thompson, Kenneth. 1998. *Moral Panics*. London: Routledge.

Timmermans, Stefan and Iddo Tavory. 2014. *Abductive Analysis: Theorizing Qualitative Research*. Chicago, IL: University of Chicago Press.

Townsley, Eleanor. 2011. "Intellectuals, media and the public sphere," pp. 284–317 in Jeffrey C. Alexander, Ronald N. Jacobs, and Philip Smith, eds., *The Oxford Handbook of Cultural Sociology*. New York: Oxford University Press.

Trachtenberg, Joshua. 1961. *The Devil and the Jews: The Medieval Conception of the Jew and Its Relation to Modern Anti-Semitism*. Cleveland, NY: World Jewish Publication Society.

Treas, Judith. 2010. "The great American recession: Sociological insights on blame and pain." *Sociological Perspectives* 53(1): 3–18.

Turner, Victor. 1982. *From Ritual to Theatre: The Human Seriousness of Play*. Baltimore, MD: PAJ Press.

Turner, Victor. 1987. *The Anthropology of Performance*. New York: PAJ Press.

Wagner-Pacifici, Robin. 1986. *The Moro Morality Play: Terrorism as Social Drama*. Chicago, IL: University of Chicago Press.

Wagner-Pacifici, Robin. 2010. "Theorizing the restlessness of events." *American Journal of Sociology* 115(5): 1351–86.

Wagner-Pacifici, Robin. 2017. *What Is an Event?* Chicago, IL: University of Chicago Press.

Walzer, Michael. 1984. *Spheres of Justice*. New York: Basic Books.

Weber, Max. 1927 [1904–5]. *The Protestant Ethic and the Spirit of Capitalism*. New York: Charles Scribner's Sons.

Weber, Max. 1978. *Economy and Society*. Berkeley: University of California Press.

Weber, Max. 1958a [1946]. "Religious rejections of the world and their directions," pp. 323–59 in Hans Gerth and C. Wright Mills, eds., *From Max Weber: Essays in Sociology*. New York: Oxford University Press.

Weber, Max. 1958b [1946]. "The Social Psychology of the World Religions," pp. 267–301 in Hans Gerth and C. Wright Mills, eds., *From Max Weber: Essays in Sociology*. New York: Oxford University Press.

White, Michael D. and Karen J. Terry. 2008. "Child sexual abuse in the Catholic Church: Revisiting the rotten apples explanation." *Criminal Justice and Behavior* 35(5): 658–78.

Wilkes, Paul. 2002. "The reformer." *New Yorker*, September 2: 50–4, 103–5.

Williams, James W. 2008. "The lessons of 'Enron': Media accounts, corporate crimes, and financial markets." *Theoretical Criminology* 12(4): 471–99.

Williams, Mark T. 2010. *Uncontrolled Risk*. New York: McGraw Hill.

Woodward, Carl and Bob Bernstein. 1974. *All the President's Men*. New York: Simon & Schuster.

Wright, Katie. 2014. "Childhood, public inquiries and late modernity," pp. 1–10 in B. West, ed., *Challenging Identities, Institutions, and Communities: Proceedings of the Australian Sociological Association*. Adelaide: University of South Australia. https://tasa.org.au/wp-content/uploads/2014/12/Wright.pdf.

Zangrando, Robert L. 1980. *The NAACP Crusades against Lynching, 1909–1950*. Philadelphia, PA: Temple University Press.

Zelizer, Viviana. 1985. *Pricing the Priceless Child*. New York: Basic Books.

# Index